edited by Mel Watkins
with
drawings by David Brown

Barry Beckham

Cecil Brown

Ed Bullins

Carole Clemmons

George Davis

Nikki Giovanni

David Henderson

Franklin Jackson

Alicia Johnson

George Kent

Julius Lester

Reginald Major

Shane Stevens

Edgar White

William Morrow & Company, Inc.
New York
1971

Mel Watkins

David Brown

George Kent

David Henderson

Ed Bullins

George Davis

Carole Clemmons

Barry Beckham

Julius Lester

Reginald Major

Shane Stevens

Nikki Giovanni

Edgar White

Franklin Jackson

Alicia Johnson

Cecil Brown

Contents

Introduction

In the late nineteen fifties and early sixties black Americans responded to their plight as second-class citizens with massive protests and appeals. Faced with the society's intransigence, the late sixties saw more militant and violent reactions and, also, the reawakening and widespread acceptance of black political nationalism. This black upsurgence and thrust for equality on the political front has dominated America's domestic scene for the past two decades. Along with United States involvement in Indo-China, it has precipitated the greatest social upheaval and polarization of United States citizenry since the Civil War. Now, as the seventies begin, black Americans find themselves, along with other segments of the society (most notably the young), involved in a game of domestic brinksmanship: the attempt to transform the "American Dream" into a workable human reality before reactionaries transform it into a brutal and overt police state.

MEL WATKINS

The events of the past two decades have also culminated in Black America's reawakening to, and acceptance of, cultural nationalism. According to many black intellectuals, in its depth and intensity, it outstrips any such movement among blacks in the past. This is as it should be, for as the hiatus between American rhetoric and deeds has broadened, the traditional quest for integration—which has meant the eradication of one's blackness—has been exposed as a cul-de-sac. Afro-Americans en masse have turned to an examination and exploration of their own heritage and roots in the hope of establishing their identities and revitalizing and developing their communities. The consequences of this reactivated interest in the dynamics and unique character of black life may be seen in events such as the recent proliferation of black drama and poetry groups, but, more important, they are revealed in the pride and courage that are now seen in the faces of many Afro-American children.

It is in this social and political context that the first issue of *Black Review* appears. Its aim is to provide a platform from which various aspects of black culture may be examined and discussed and a showcase in which the works of black writers and poets, particularly the young, may be displayed. It is intended to encompass the wide spectrum of opinion and viewpoint that exists in the black community and allow discourse between dissident factions. But its primary function is to further the black man's independent analysis and defining of black American culture, in the hope that it be better understood and more richly developed. Nonblack writers will appear when it is felt that their examination of some aspect of their own culture illuminates an interrelated aspect of black life. Toward these ends, the selections for the initial issue of *Black Review* have been chosen.

Fiction in this issue is provided by novelist Barry Beckham, playwright Ed Bullins, George Davis and Franklin J. Jackson. The poetry contributors are David Henderson, Carole Clemmons and Alicia L. Johnson; Edgar White has a one-act play.

George E. Kent has contributed an essay on the contemporary relevance of Richard Wright, and novelist Cecil Brown has written on singer James Brown. Julius Lester, Reginald Major, Shane Stevens and Nikki Giovanni have contributed essays focused on the revolutionary possibilities in contemporary American society.

Finally, it should be stated that the success of a publication depends in large part on its responsiveness to its readership; therefore manuscripts as well as letters and comments will be welcomed and appreciated. Then, hopefully, *Black Review* may contribute significantly to the understanding and expansion of the black consciousness that has already begun.

A View of the Artist

David Scott Brown, the illustrator of this book, is a graduate of Pratt Institute and is employed on the art staff of *The New York Times*. His work has been displayed in group shows in the New York area and in several one-man exhibitions. When asked about his view of *art* he made the following reply:

Jazz is an interest of mine (I play a little) and when I portray a jazz musician I try to capture, through color, the rhythms of jazz as well as the sound itself. This typifies my "style" of art. For me, art is a matter of mood and feeling, line and color projecting movement and emotion.

DAVID BROWN

Richard Wright: Blackness and the Adventure of Western Culture

In the nineteen fifties literary opinion makers were in a great hurry to clear the stage of Richard Wright and to make room for more *art-conscious* black writers. Critical generalizations and intuitive judgments hardened into critical party lines, and since the stormy sociological surface of Wright's works was the focus of the liberal establishment, there was a tendency to insist that the issues which he raised were completely topical—issues, it was thought, that were being speedily resolved by liberal emotions, New Deal legislation, Supreme Court edicts, NAACP persistence, and Freedom Marches. Then suddenly, the halo of the integration struggle sizzled with third-degree burns in the flames of a hundred cities. If those bewildered and snarling black faces that rose up from television screens to haunt our minds and souls were not the exact replicas of Bigger Thomas, his family and friends, they sure sounded like real close kin.

GEORGE KENT

Thus Richard Wright now seems relevant. Once criticized for committing himself to deprived and inarticulate heroes whose sensibilities could not possibly grasp the big picture, Wright now appears to have anticipated the urban upheavals, the alienation and the violence of our times (an achievement which was beyond the capacity of sociologists). Indeed, he is yet the lone black writer to look so carefully into the psychology of the ordinary mass of black minds, and to understand that when their stake in the dignity of man was no longer legally programmed out of existence, a soulless technology would have sufficient rhythm to complete the job with no loss of momentum.

So much for contemporary relevance.

It is important for leading us to the discovery that insufficiently recognized themes emerge from the vital depths of Wright's works: the growth of consciousness and reclaiming the heritage of man.

It is important for impelling us to render the tribute due a writer of Wright's great creative talent: close critical engagement and thorough absorption.

So impelled, we ask what is to be done in the study of Wright? The answer that comes back to us is, "Everything."

I shall try to focus upon three sources of Wright's power: his double-consciousness, his personal tension and his dramatic articulation of black and white culture.

His double-consciousness and personal tension can be discussed at the same time, since one flows into and activates the other. His personal tension springs from a stubborn self—conscious of victimization, but obsessed with its right to a full engagement of universal forces and to a reaping of the fruits due from the engagement. This right may be called the heritage of man. And his double-consciousness is not unlike what W. E. B. Du Bois, in *The Souls of Black Folk*, described as the black man's sense of being something defined and imprisoned by the myths of whites and at war with his consciousness of American citizenship and its supposed rights. The consciousness of American citizenship ignites aspiration, but impels the artist to look worshipfully upon the general

American culture and to devalue his condition and that of his people, even when he is conscious of their beauty:

> The innate love of harmony and beauty that set the ruder souls of his people a-dancing and a-singing raised but confusion and doubt in the soul of the black artist; for the beauty revealed to him was the soul beauty of a race which his larger audience despised, and he could not articulate the message of another people.

Frantz Fanon, in *Black Skins, White Masks,* says simply that the black is overdetermined from without and gives this dramatic picture: "I progress by crawling. And already I am being dissected under white eyes, the only real eyes." In literature, the war of the two consciousnesses sometimes drives for an art that is "only incidentally" about Negroes, if it is about them at all; in which case the writer carefully reduces his particularism (the tensioned details of the black experience) and hustles to the "universal" (usually the culturally conditioned Western version). Other choices: to portray the exoticism that satisfies the symbolic needs of whites; to plead the humanity of blacks before a white audience; and, lately, to dig out and address a black audience, regarding its condition and its beauty. Within the concept of double-consciousness, it will be seen that Wright was both the cunning artificer and the victim.

But first, his personal tension, without which he may not have created at all, a tension, not really separable from the double-consciousness, that is one great source of his creative power. A slight handicap here, from the angle of scholarly documentation—the main source for information concerning Wright's early youth is still *Black Boy,* a great autobiography, but one whose claim to attention is the truth of the artist, and not that of the factual reporter. Both Ralph Ellison and Constance Webb, Wright's biographer, have identified incidents which Wright did not personally experience, incidents from folk tradition. I see no great to-do to be made over Wright's artistic license, since folk tradition is the means by which a group expresses its deepest truths. Thus the picture, if not all the pieces, is essentially true.

What *Black Boy* reveals is that more than any other major black writer, Wright, in his youth, was close to the black masses—and in the racially most repressive state in the union, Mississippi. Worse still, Wright received violent suppression without the easement provided by the moral bewilderment and escapism so available in black culture. Such institutionalized instruments of bewilderment as the otherworldly religion, the smiling side of the "good" white folks, sex, liquor and the warmth of the folk culture formed no sustaining portion of his psychic resources. Parents, whose complicity in oppression made for physical security in the South of the pre- and post-World War I periods, were in Wright's case ineffectual. His father was a zero. His mother —a woman bearing up under tensions from the terrors of the daily world, abandonment by a shiftless husband and painful and disabling sickness—was hard pressed by Wright and her own tough-minded honesty. Under a persistent barrage of questions concerning black life, answers escaped her lips that merely confirmed the boy's sense of embattlement in a world of naked terror; first, for example, explaining that a white man did not whip a black boy because the black boy was his son, she then sharpened a distinction: "The 'white' man did not *whip* the 'black' boy. He *beat* the 'black' boy."

Constance Webb, in *Richard Wright*, states Wright's conscious purpose: "to use himself as a symbol of all the brutality and cruelty wreaked upon the black man by the Southern environment." By depressing his middle-class background, Miss Webb continues, he would create a childhood that would be representative of most Negroes. Both the power of the autobiography and its flaws develop from Wright's single-minded intention. Actually, for much of the work, his strategy is to posit a self-beyond-culture—that is, the self as biological fact, a very tough biological fact, indeed. A cosmic self, which reaches out naturally (though in twisted and violent patterns) for the beauty and nobility of life. The self is battered by the white racist culture, and, for the most part, by a survival-oriented black culture that counters the impulse to rebelliousness and individuality by puritanical repressiveness, escapism and base submission. That is, black culture suppressed the individual in order to protect the group from white assault. The dramatic rendering of these forces and the stubborn persistence of the outsider comprise the major strategy of the book.

And out of that strategy comes an overwhelming impact. Tension, raw violence and impending violence, which evoke, psychologically, a nightmare world in the light of day. The autobiography's first great subject is the growth of consciousness, the stages of which are communicated by statements of the reactions of self to preceding events. In confronting a racist America the black boy's consciousness learns to hide its responses and to pursue its aspirations by secret means. It is damaged for life, but it has avoided becoming a natural product of the system: the stunted, degraded, shuffling black, almost convinced of its own inferiority and the godlike power of whites. In the latter part of the book, through reading rebellious works, the consciousness of that other self —the white-defined Negro-victim—loses ground to the consciousness of self as American: heir to the energy-releasing resources of the American myth and the so-called period of Enlightenment. A desperate hope is created.

Thus *Black Boy*'s second great subject: the disinherited attempting to reclaim the heritage of Modern Man.

Black Boy is a great social document, but it could easily have been greater. Its simple naturalistic form at first knocks the reader off balance, but then comes reflection. Its universe of terror is little relieved by those moments of joy that usually glide like silent ancestral spirits into the grimmest childhood. To account artistically for the simple survival of the narrator is difficult. Except for the "cultural transfusion" that the narrator receives near the end, Wright gives little artistic emphasis to cultural supports. The careful reader will pick up, here and there, scattered clues. For example, the extended family, with all its shortcomings, shows a desperate energy and loyalty. Reading was an early feeder of his imaginative life, and the role of his mother in supplying imaginative and emotional help was crucial. In *Black Boy*, the dramatic form does not, in itself, give her a decisive role, but the beatings, teasings, grim love and sporadic periods of silent understanding imply an unorthodox devotion. The narrator reveals something of the sort in stating the impact of her sickness upon him:

> Already there had crept into her speech a halting, lisping quality that, though I did not know it, was the shadow of her future. I was more conscious of my mother now than I had ever been and I was already able to feel what being completely without her would mean.

There were important facets of ordinary black life, which Wright did not understand because he saw them as an outsider or from the point of view of embattled adolescence. His father was simply the peasant-victim, with a life shaped by the rhythms of the seasons—a classification very likely to have been derived from his Marxian studies. In Memphis, Wright (or the narrator) meets Mrs. Moss, a spontaneously warm and generous black woman, with an equally warm and spontaneous daughter, Bess. Bess likes Richard and, in no time flat, wishes to marry him. The narrator is aware of her qualities, but ascribes their source to what he was later to understand as "the peasant mentality."

Yet this warm spontaneity, as much as the warped puritanism of his own environment, was a value bulwarked and preserved by the embattled black cultural tradition—not by nature or the rhythm of the seasons. Thus the utter bleakness of black life, its lack of tenderness, love, honor, genuine passion, which Wright in a now famous passage in the second chapter of *Black Boy* noted as general characteristics, were partly reflections of his immediate home life and surroundings: "I had come from a home where feelings were never expressed, except in rage or religious dread, where each member of the household lived locked in his own dark world, and the light that shone out of this child's heart [Bess's] . . . blinded me."

Personal tension and the double-consciousness. In response to white definitions, Wright was able to say to whites that he formed an equation not known in their definitions. Regarding his people, he was able to say that they are much like you define them but you, and not nature, are responsible. If today, this no longer seems enough to say, or even to be free of a certain adolescent narcissism, we can at least concentrate upon what insights should have been available to Wright during his time. If Wright in *Black Boy* seems too much concerned with warfare upon white definitions, it is good to remember that our growing ability to ignore them exists because the single-minded assault of Wright and others shook up the confidence of a nation and impaired their efficiency.

What can be held against him is that he seemed to have had little awareness that black life, on its own terms, has also the measure of beauty and grandeur granted those who are often defeated but not destroyed. It would be good here to know more about his reading, especially works written by black men. How startling, for example, to learn from Constance Webb that at the age of thirty-two, in 1940, Wright had not read Booker T. Washington's *Up from Slavery*. In a footnote to Chapter 13 of *Richard Wright,* Miss Webb states:

> Wright was almost ashamed to admit that he had never read *Up from Slavery.* He had escaped being educated in Negro institutions and never got around to reading those books which everyone was supposed to read. He did know that the greatest split among educated Negroes of a generation or so ago was over Washington's proposals.

Miss Webb is valiant, but the explanation is lame. That very boyhood which Wright was attempting to understand in *Black Boy* depends, for proper dimension, upon an intimate knowledge of Booker T. Washington and W. E. B. Du Bois and of the issues with which they grappled. Ironically, by 1903, Du Bois in "Of Our Spiritual Strivings," *The Souls of Black Folk,* had already defined the problems and the danger which Wright (born in 1908) would confront as a writer. Aside from such considerations, it would hardly seem that a person as obsessed with black problems as Wright was would require an education in Negro institutions to put him in touch with the major figures in his history.

The truth is probably that having caught a breath of life from the literature of revolt against the American small town and from Marxian dialectics Wright was overimpressed with their efficiency as tools to explore the privacy and complexity of the black environment. Certainly, Ellison, in 1941, described a system that Wright used for mastering culture that was double-edged and required wariness. Ellison praised Wright for translating the American responses that he heard whites express into terms with which to express the life of Bigger Thomas in *Native Son*. In an article that appeared in *New Masses* in 1945, Ellison credited Wright with thus building up within himself "tensions and disciplines . . . impossible within the relaxed, semi-peasant environs of American Negro life." Now such a system can immediately broaden and deepen perspective, but it also carries an obvious payload of distortion. In this regard, it is interesting to note that Ellison, who, in 1945, was obviously disturbed by Wright's famous description of black life as bleak and barren, in *Shadow and Act* said later that it was simply a paraphrase of Henry James's description, in his *Hawthorne*, of "those items of high civilization which were absent from American life during Hawthorne's day, and which seemed so necessary in order for the novelist to function." One might add that the hard and sharp articulate terms of the black narrator's individualism and rationalism in *Black Boy* seem occasionally to be imports from Northern urban middle-class culture. Neither the folk black culture of the nineteen twenties nor the general Southern culture allowed a childhood to escape the compulsion toward an almost superstitious display of forms of reverence for its elders—even when "reality" gave no justification for them. The rebellion against such a compulsion would, if natively expressed, have been less confident and articulate, more in the forms of silence, sullenness and guilty outbursts.

In *Black Boy*, the young Richard Wright's impulse to individuality has already begun to engage the dominant forms of Western culture. It promises arms for the freedom of both the black artist and his people. On the other hand, the forms have, for him, their dead-end streets. Individualism in Western culture ranges from rugged activity to imprisonment in one's own subjectivity. While enabling one to escape the confines of a survival-oriented folk culture and to take arms against the West's racism, Western cultural forms threaten to subtly transform the emotional and psychic reflexes, so that while the black writer's status is one of alienation, his deepest consciousness is that of the exaggerated Westerner.

In successive autobiographical statements Wright's alienation was apparent. In "The Man Who Went to Chicago," from *Eight Men*, the picture is one of alienated man trying to express impulses which the forms of Western culture are supposedly dedicated to promoting: the triumph of the human individual (as Fanon termed it), of curiosity and of beauty. But in Chicago, the capitalistic culture was giving no public sanction to the possession of such qualities by black men, and "adjusted" blacks were themselves an obstacle, as they vied for status in their misery.

Within the Communist Party, as reflected in "I Tried to Be a Communist," Wright found the "triumph of the human individual" balked on ideological grounds. As to the racial thing, one leftist writer confessed, while recruiting Wright for a Communist-front group, that "We write articles about Negroes, but we never see any Negroes." When it came to getting Wright a room in the New York City of 1935, the Communists went through the same foot-shuffling affected by other white Americans, and, in order to attend the Communist-sponsored conference, Wright, himself, found a room in the Negro Y.M.C.A., miles from the site of the conference.

Wright, a very big man, was aware that the Communists had no understanding of the depths of the lives of black men. But Marxism was *the* dynamic philosophy for social change. Where else was he to go? Meanwhile, his life reflected, in an eighth-grade dropout's mastery of world culture, the great Western ideal: the expression of the individual life as revolutionary will. The process jerked uptight his emotional and moral reflexes. When he confronted African culture in *Black Power* or met representatives of non-Western cultures, he was both the alienated black man and the exaggerated Westerner, and was at once sympathetic and guiltily sniffy, according to Constance Webb. The fit of the two is uneasy. In *Black Power, Pagan Spain, The Color Curtain,* and *White Man, Listen!,* nonfictional works, the personality behind the print ranges from that of a bright but somewhat snippish Western tourist to that of a Western schoolmarm, although his ideas are most frequently interesting and provocative.

But Wright remained embattled.

And in the nineteen fifties, in the novel *The Outsider,* he was raising the question as to whether the Western game had not lost all vitality.

II

For Richard Wright the job of writing was most serious and his struggle was very great. In an article in *New Challenge,* "Blue-Print for Negro Writing," he saw blacks as essentially a separate nation and felt that the job of the black writer was to create the values by which his race would live and die. However, he argued that ultimately a nationalist perspective did not go far enough, and that having broadened his consciousness through an understanding of the nationalistic folklore of his people, the black writer must transcend nationalism and transform his own personality through the Marxian conception of reality.

Now Harold Cruse in *The Crisis of the Negro Intellectual* has ably pointed out that the American imported and unadapted Marxism was a dead-end street, since it had no conception of the black reality nor any real intention of acquiring one. As I have indicated, Wright was not unaware of the myopia of American Marxists. His positive gain was sufficient psychological distance from the American middle-class oriented cultural patterns to articulate perspectives and symbols of the black and white cultures. This gave him, at least, a version of the total American reality as it relates to blacks. Although Wright had qualified his Marxist stance by stating that Marxism was the bare bones upon which the black writer must graft the flesh, he did ask that the writer mold Negro folklore "with the concepts that move and direct the forces of history today," that is, with Marxism. The negative effects of this Marxism, as well as the emphatic convictions that derived from psychology and the social sciences, were that the very lights they provided for gaining power over certain aspects of black humanity, by their very glare, blinded him to others.

Take that fine group of short stories that comprise *Uncle Tom's Children*. On a first reading, the reader is overwhelmed by the sheer power of naturalistic form, out of which several stories explode upon him. In "Big Boy Leaves Home," Big Boy and his gang are discovered by a Southern white woman bathing in the nude in a Southern white man's creek. (The black man and the white woman are a Negro folklore theme.) Startled when they come toward her to get their clothes, she screams. Her nearby escort shoots and kills two of the boys, and Big Boy wrests the gun from him and kills him. With the help of the folk community and his family, Big Boy escapes, but his friend Bobo is brutally lynched by a mob. From his hiding place Big Boy witnesses the deed. He escapes the following morning in a truck bound for Chicago.

The story has been very justly admired. In the nineteen thirties when the story first appeared the very type of lynching it described was horribly so much more than a mere literary reality. Black men, remembering the wariness with which they stepped around such women in real life and that lingering dread of being trapped with them in some unstructured situation where neither "racial etiquette" nor rational chat would absolve, could read and feel the stomach gone awry. Also that high irreverence of boyhood smashed up against the System is so well pictured; the dialogue is so full of life, and the folk culture so carefully evoked—who could resist? Add to this powerful scenes and narrative drive.

But then, a serious flaw. Wright's chief interest is in Big Boy—in his raw revolutionary will to survive and prevail. So that Wright forgets that youth does not experience the shooting down of two comrades and the horrible lynching of a third, without a sea change in its nature. But Big Boy remains simply preoccupied with physical well-being and casually explains how it went with his comrade Bobo: "They burnt im . . . Will, ah wan some water; mah throat's like fire."

"Down by the Riverside" continues the emphasis upon the will to survive, although Mann, the main character, is killed by soldiers under emergency flood conditions. Mann is determined to get his pregnant wife to a doctor and his family to the hills away from flood waters that already swirl at his cabin door. In a stolen boat, he is forced to kill a white man. Mann pits his will against nature and whites. It is a brilliant but losing battle and he knows well before the events that he will be captured and killed.

He expresses will by determining the moment when he will die. In this way, he briefly affirms for the universe that Mann existed:

> Yes, now, he would die! He would die before he would let them kill him. Ah'll die fo they kill me! Ah'll *die* . . . He ran straight to the right, through the trees, in the direction of the water. He heard a shot.

Although he is killed by the soldiers, they have been forced to accept the time that he offers.

With "Long Black Song," the third story, the focus is shifted. Silas, the character representing individual will, does not appear until the second half of the story. Wright instead focuses upon Sarah, Silas's wife, a person conceived of as sunk-in-nature or as undifferentiated nature. The shift destroys the simple story line which Wright has followed. Blacks, uncommitted to struggle, in the earlier stories, were backstaged or absent.

Sarah, on the other hand, as a black person not emerged from nature, requires a creative energy to lift her from the category of stereotype which Wright was unable to give her. One has to see her as earth goddess or as the stereotype of loose sexuality. Since Silas's violent war with whites and his obvious needs and heroic struggle claim the sympathy of the reader, the symbols that have given Sarah a tenuous stature as earth goddess, above the wars of black and white men, crumble, and she appears as mere mindless stupidity and sensuality.

In her actions Sarah resists Western clock time. The sole clock in the house is out of repair. In an obviously symbolic action, her baby is unpacified when she holds him up to the sun (nature's time), but quietens when she allows him to beat upon the clock (Western time). She declares that they need no clock. "We just don't need no time, mistah." Wright gears her responses to images of the season and its rhythms.

Dreaming secretly of Tom, a man with a similar emotional structure, Sarah is seduced by a white salesman, whose music and personality evoke her maternal feelings and a sense of harmonious nature. Silas, her husband, upon discovering betrayal, kills the salesman and other white men. Again the choice factor of the stern-willed: Facing a lynch mob, Silas insists upon determining the mode of his death by remaining in his burning house, which the mob has set on fire.

Silas breaks out in one powerful nationalistic chant against the way the cards are stacked against him as a black man in the universe. He has accepted the world of time, materialistic struggle and manipulation of nature. He has worked for ten years to become the owner of his farm. Yet the tone and terms of his chant imply that the dread of the day of reckoning had long been on his mind: "He began to talk to no one in particular; he simply stood over the dead white man and talked out of his life, out of a deep and final sense that now it was all over and nothing could make any difference."

> "The white folks ain never gimme a chance! They ain never give no black man a chance! there ain nothin in your whole life yuh kin keep from 'em. They take yo lan. They take yo women! N' then they take yo life."

In addition, he is stabbed in the back by "Mah own blood," i.e., his wife. At bottom, Silas is concerned about the meaning of his life.

This nationalistic base is also a part of the two preceding stories. In "Big Boy Leaves Home" it is tacitly assumed. The folk elders' unspoken assumptions, the quickness with which they devise Big Boy's escape, and the white supremacy assumptions with which whites instantly and almost casually commit the most horrible violence, reflect nationalist stances. In "Down by the Riverside," a part of the same nationalistic assumptions are operative, and Mann expresses a lament for the failure of himself and others to live up to the nationalistic implications of their lives:

> For a split second he was there among those blunt and hazy black faces looking silently and fearfully at the white folks take some poor black man away. Why don they help me? Yet he knew they would not and could not help him, even as he in times past had not helped other black men being taken by the white folks to their death.

In a vital creative formula, Wright has thus combined the idea of revolutionary will, embryonic nationalism, and Negro folklore molded into a martial stance.

The pattern is continued in the last two stories, which differ from the first group by bringing the Communist movement into the picture and having the individual will relate to the group will. "Fire and Cloud" has the black minister Taylor to lead black and white workers in a march upon a Southern town, which has refused to relieve their hunger. At first Taylor's motivations are religious impulses and a concept of nature as communal. The tilling of the land brings organic satisfaction of great depth. But the whites have taken the land and confiscated nature. Taylor's will is strong. He endures vicious beatings by whites and learns that he must get with the people if the problem is to be solved.

The last story, "Bright and Morning Star," is superior to "Fire and Cloud," because it more carefully investigates the inner psychology of An Sue, a mother of communists, who gives up the image of Christ by which she has formerly shrunk from the world. Her nationalistic impulse is in her distrust for white comrades, a feeling which her son has enthusiastically transcended. An Sue, however, is all too prophetic. Booker, a poor white communist informer, tricks her into giving him the names of comrades, although her intuition sees him in the image of the oppressor, the "white mountain."

Now in order to see Johnny Boy, whom the mob has captured, and confirm her suspicions about Booker, she goes to the mob scene "lika nigga woman wid mah windin sheet t git mah dead son." In the sheet she conceals a gun. Defiantly refusing to make her captured son inform, she endures his being maimed; then as Booker begins to inform, she kills him. She and her son are then killed by the mob, although "She gave up as much of her life as she could before they took it from her."

The nationalist impulse thus overrides both escapist religion and communism. She is between two worlds without the benefit of the "grace" that either might confer. The impulse that sustains her defiance is more than nationalist; it is that of revolutionary will, the demand for the right to give final shape to the meaning of one's life. In a word, like all the heroic characters of *Uncle Tom's Children*, her choice is existential. The device of the winding sheet, with which she asserts her will, will be recognized as part of a well-known Negro folklore story.

As Wright's fictional scene moved to the urban ghetto, he encountered a new challenge because, unlike the Southern mob, sheriff or plantation owner, the forces that attacked the lives of black people were so often abstract and impersonal. Yet out of the urban area were to come the most prophetic images relevant to the ordinary black man in the ghetto.

Although *Lawd Today* was first published in 1963, a statement in the bibliographical section of Constance Webb's *Richard Wright* notes that it "was probably written sometime between 1935 and 1937." Constance Webb speaks of his working on a novel about post-office workers during the summer of 1935. The book does have something of an exploratory air about it, and it certainly does not immediately connect its wires to ideology or resound in defense of blacks. I think that critics have been offended by the brutality and lower-depth quality, which its black characters project. Wright's flaming defense of blacks and indictment of whites had filled the vision of even mild-mannered black critics and given them the benefit of a genteel catharsis; therefore, it was very easy to miss the more negative attitudes that he held in regard to black life.

Yet *Lawd Today* is very important in the study of Richard Wright for several reasons. It defines at least an essential part of black life, points up the importance of the inscriptions from other writings as aids to understanding his intentions, and enables us to see Wright examining a slice of black life practically on its own terms.

In addition to Wright's strictures on black life in *Black Boy* (cultural barrenness, lack of tenderness and genuine passion), there had also appeared the statement that "I know that Negroes had never been allowed to catch the full spirit of Western Civilization, that they lived somehow in it but not of it." *Lawd Today* addresses itself to this situation. The title *Lawd Today,* a folk exclamation on confronting the events of the day, is to express a people who have not been able to make their life their own, who must live "from day to day." And as Conrad Kent Rivers put it in his poem on Wright: "To Live from Day to Day is not to live at all."

To compound the problem: Wright was perfectly capable of seeing emptiness as characteristic of the life of the ordinary white worker. In "The Man Who Went to Chicago," his white female coworkers in a restaurant exposed "their tawdry dreams, their simple hopes, their home lives, their fear of feeling anything deeply . . ." Although they were casually kind and impersonal, "they knew nothing of hate and fear, and strove instinctively to avoid all passion." Their lives were totally given to striving "for petty goals, the trivial material prizes of American life." To become more than children, they would have to include in their personalities "a knowledge of lives such as I lived and suffered containedly." Wright is on his way to describing a shallowly optimistic America, one that avoided the tragic encounter and the knowledge to be derived therefrom, one that excluded blacks from "the entire tide and direction of American culture," although they are "an organic part of the nation . . ."

A similarity, yes, and yet a difference. Wright seems to see ordinary white life by its intrinsic relationship to Western technology, as pulled into some semblance of order— one that is sufficient for superficial living, elementary assertion of will and materialistic acquisitiveness. On the other hand, Saunders Redding comments perceptively on one of Wright's objections to black life in an essay that appeared in *Anger and Beyond*: Wright knew "that survival for the Negro depended upon his not making choices, upon his ability to adapt to choices (the will of others) made for him. He hated this . . ." In his introduction to the 1945 edition of St. Clair Drake and Horace R. Cayton's *Black Metropolis*, Wright more fully describes conditions which he feels deprive modern man of deep organic satisfaction and program the stunted and frenzied lives of blacks.

As an expression of this extreme frustration, *Lawd Today* deserves a separate and more careful analysis than I can here give to it. Its universe provides its chief character, Jake Jackson, a Mississippi migrant, and his friends no true self-consciousness. It is a universe of violence, magic, quack medicine, numbers playing and dreambooks, roots and herbs, cheap movies, tuberculosis, and venereal disease, hard liquor and sex and corrupt politics. The relation between Jake Jackson and his wife Lil is that of warfare; the book begins with Jake's brutal beating of her, and it ends with Jake's drunken attempt to beat her again, an event that sees her, in self-defense, knocking him unconscious.

"Lawd, I wish I was dead," she [Lil] sobbed softly.
Outside an icy wind swept around the corner of the building, whining and moaning like an idiot in a deep black pit.

The brutal relations of Jake and Lil provide the one-day frame for the book. The only real value represented is the rough and ready fellowship between Jake and his friends— Al, whose pride stems from his membership in a national guard unit that breaks up strikes and leftist gatherings; Bob, who suffers throughout the story from a bad case of gonorrhea; and Slim, whose body is wracked with tuberculosis. Jake knows that something is missing from his life, but he can't pin it down. So he and his comrades turn to whatever will jolt their bodies into a brief illusion of triumphant living.

Wright uses several external devices in order to make his intentions apparent. For rather heavy-handed irony, he has the events take place on Lincoln's Birthday. The radio delivers a steady barrage of talk about the war that freed the slaves while Jake and his friends, spiritually lost and enslaved in urban society, fumble through the events of the day. Part I bears the inscription taken from Van Wyck Brooks's *America's Coming-of-Age*: ". . . a vast Sargasso Sea—a prodigious welter of unconscious life, swept by groundswells of half-conscious emotion . . ." The inscription is obviously well-chosen, and is to be applied to the lives of Jake and his friends. Part II is entitled "Squirrel Cage," a section in which the characters' actions are no more fruitful than that of caged animals. An inscription from Waldo Frank's *Our America* speaks of the lives of men and women as "some form of life that has hardened but not grown, and over which the world has passed. . . ." Part III takes both its title, "Rat's Alley," and its inscription from T. S. Eliot's *Wasteland*: ". . . But at my back in a cold blast I hear/The rattle of the bones, and chuckle spread from ear to ear." Thus the title headings and the inscriptions alert the reader to the themes of artificially stunted and sterile lives, half-conscious and inarticulate, and force a wider reference to their universe. Something very big and nasty is indeed biting the characters in *Lawd Today*, but it is part of the theme of the book that, though one character prays and most of the others beg, borrow and "ball," they cannot name the water that would relieve their wasteland.

In concentrating upon simply presenting the lives and their surroundings, Wright displays gifts that are not the trademarks of his other novels. Sensational incidents do not threaten the principle of proportion or make melodrama an end in itself. Of all things, Wright displays, in his opening portrait of Jake Jackson, a talent for biting satire! Humor, so limited in other works, is often wildly raucous. The gift for portraying extended scenes, apparent in other works and so important to the novelist, is still marvelously in evidence. So also is Wright's great talent for the recording of speech rhythms and color. In the character Al's narrative of a masochistic black woman, Wright even does credit to the tall-story tradition.

But his most astonishing performance is Section IV of "Squirrel Cage," in which, for thirty pages, all speeches are anonymous and the postal workers render communally their inner life and feelings.

> They had worked in this manner for so many years that they took one another for granted; their common feelings were a common knowledge. And when they talked it was more like thinking aloud than speaking for purposes of communication. Clusters of emotion, dim accretions of instinct and tradition rose to the surface of their consciousness like dead bodies floating and swollen upon a night sea.

Despite the negative simile about dead bodies, the speeches form a poem, a device which breaks the novel's tight realism and gives its rendering power a new dimension. It is strange that Wright did not develop the technique further, since his naturalism, in order to fully encompass his reach, required the supplement of his own intrusive commentary.

Lawd Today enlarges our perspective on *Native Son*, for it creates the universe of Bigger Thomas in terms more dense than the carefully chosen symbolic reference points of *Native Son*. The continuity of Wright's concerns stand out with great clarity and depth. Running through all Wright's works and thoroughly pervading his personality is his identification with and rejection of the West, and his identification with and rejection of the conditions of black life. *Lawd Today* is primarily concerned with the latter.

In *Native Son*, Wright's greatest work, he returned to the rebel outsider, the character with revolutionary will and the grit to make existential choices. Bigger Thomas, like the heroic characters of *Uncle Tom's Children*, finally insists upon defining the meaning of his life: ". . . What I killed for, I am," cries Bigger at the end of his violent and bloody life.

Wright early establishes the myth of the heritage of man, Western man, as a counterpoint to the disinherited condition of Bigger Thomas, a Southern black migrant with an eighth-grade education. In the first section of the novel, Bigger expresses his frustration by violent and cowardly reactions and by references to the rituals of power and freedom that he envies. What does he wish to happen, since he complains that nothing happens in his universe? "Anything, Bigger said with a wide sweep of his dingy palm, a sweep that included all the possible activities of the world."

> Then their eyes [Bigger's and his gang's] were riveted; a slate colored pigeon swooped down to the middle of the steel car tracks and began strutting to and fro with ruffled feathers, its fat neck bobbing with regal pride. A street car rumbled forward and the pigeon rose swiftly through the air on wings stretched so taut and sheer that Bigger could see the god of the sun through their translucent tips. He tilted his head and watched the slate-colored bird flap and wheel out of sight over the ridge of a high roof.
>
> "Now, if I could only do that," Bigger said.

Bigger, himself, instinctively realizes that a job and night school will not fundamentally alter his relationship to the universe. To the white and wealthy Mrs. Dalton's query concerning night school, his mind silently makes a vague response: "Night school was all right, but he had other plans. Well, he didn't know just what they were right now, but he was working them out." As to the job with the Daltons, it is but an extension of the System that holds him in contempt and stifles his being; the "relief" people will cut off his food and starve his family if he does not take it. Because of the resulting pressure from his family for physical comfort and survival, ". . . he felt that they had tricked him into a cheap surrender." The job and night school would have programmed his life into conformity with what Wright called the "pet nigger system," but would not have gained respect for his manhood.

Bigger Thomas and Richard Wright were after the System—not merely its pieces.

A major source of the power of *Native Son* derived from Wright's ability to articulate the relevant rituals of black and white cultures—and Bigger's response to them. These rituals emphasize the presence in culture of rational drive, curiosity, revolutionary will, individualism, self-consciousness (preoccupations of Western culture)—or their absence.

Thus blindness (shared by white and black cultures), softness, shrinking from life, escapism, otherworldliness, abjectness and surrender, are the meaning of the black cultural rituals from which Bigger recoils, and the counters with which blacks are allowed to purchase their meager allowance of shelter and bread. They contrast sharply with Bigger's (the outsider's) deep urges for freedom of gesture and spontaneous response to existence. Wright's indictment is that these negative qualities are systematically programmed into black culture by the all-powerful white oppressor.

Having murdered the white girl Mary Dalton—thus defying the imprisoning white oppressor—Bigger Thomas feels a rush of energy that makes him equal to the oppressor. He now explains his revolt against black culture. Buddy, his brother, is "soft and vague; his eyes were defenseless and their glance went only to the surface of things." Buddy is "aimless, lost, with no sharp or hard edges, like a chubby puppy." There is in him "a certain stillness, an isolation, meaninglessness."

Bigger's sister Vera "seemed to be shrinking from life with every gesture she made." His mother has religion in place of whiskey, and his girlfriend Bessie has whiskey in place of religion. In the last section of *Native Son,* his mother's epiphany is her crawling on her knees from one white Dalton to the other to beg for the life of Bigger. In "Flight," the second part of the novel, Bessie's epiphany is a prose blues complaint concerning the trap of her life, and then in a terrible sigh that surrenders to Bigger her entire will, she betrays her life completely. Finally, after Bigger is captured, a black minister epiphanizes the version of religious passivity that insured endurance of aimless and cramped life, as he unsuccessfully appeals to the captured Bigger. The gestures and rituals of the black minister are rendered with masterly brilliance.

In contrast, the symbols, rituals, and personalities of the white culture express directness, spontaneous freedom, at-homeness in the universe, will—and tyranny. While Bigger concentrates upon avoiding answering questions from the communist Jan Erlone and the liberal Mary Dalton in yes-or-no terms, he is confounded by their ability to act and speak simply and directly. In a very fine scene that evidences Wright's great novelistic talent, their very freedom and liberality dramatize his oppression and shame. Their gestures say that it is their universe. And the fact that Jan Erlone and Mary Dalton, in seconds, can, as individuals, suspend all racial restraints underlines the habitual racial rigidities ingrained in Bigger's life, which deprive him of spontaneous gesture. Oppressively, "To Bigger his kind white people were not really people; they were a sort of great natural force, like a stormy sky looming overhead, or like a deep swirling river stretching suddenly at one's feet in the dark." The white world is the "white blur," "white walls," "the snow,"—all of which place Bigger in the condition of the desperate rat with which *Native Son* begins.

The Jan Erlone–Dalton group of whites express the rituals mediated by a sufficient humanism to partially obscure their relationship to a brutal system. They inspire Bigger's hatred but also a measure of bewilderment. Even the elder Dalton can be nice because the System does the work. With one hand he functions in a company that restricts blacks to ghettos and squeezes from them high rents for rat-infested, cramped apartments; with the other, and without conscious irony, he gives substantial sums to black uplift organizations. Although Dalton's kindness cannot extend to sparing Bigger's life (since he has murdered his daughter—the flower of the system), he will prevent the ejection of Bigger's family from its rat-dominated apartment.

The liberalism of the communist Jan Erlone, his girl-friend-sympathizer Mary Dalton and the rest of the Dalton family function as esthetic rituals that create an easygoing atmosphere for sullen submission and inhibition. In the militarized zone are the racial rituals of Detective Britten bouncing Bigger's head against the wall and spitting out definitions of blacks that deny their life. Then there are the agents of the mass media, the rhetoricians, the police, and the mob.

Bigger standing equally outside the shrinking black culture and the hard-driving white culture can only feel the existential choice demanded by his compulsion toward the heritage of man shoving upward from his guts, and sense that something very terrible must happen to him. Near the end he is tortured by the knowledge that his deepest hunger is for human communion, and by his lawyer's briefly raising it as a possibility. But the mirage is soon exposed and he must warm himself by the bleak embers of his hard-won and lonely existential knowledge: ". . . what I killed for, I am!"

It is part of the greatness of *Native Son* that it survives a plethora of flaws. For example, despite Wright's indictment of white society, he shows in his major fiction little knowledge that while black life is stifled by brutality, the private realities of white life find it increasingly impossible for a white to free himself from the imprisoning blandishments of a neurotic culture. His failure to portray this fact, although we have seen that he had some understanding of it, makes it seem that Bigger's problems would have been solved by his entry into the white world. The great engagement of the universe that rages through the first and second parts of the novel sputters, at points, in the third part while Wright scores debater's points on jobs, housing and equal opportunity. The famous courtroom speech that the attorney Max makes in behalf of Bigger hardly rises above such humanitarian matters. Thus a novel that resounds in revolutionary tones descends to merely reformist modulations that would make glad the heart of a New Deal liberal.

As the theme and situations of the novel increase in density of implication, Wright is too frequently touching the reader's elbow to explain reactions and make distinctions that are too complex for Bigger to verbalize. The style, therefore, fails at crucial points. Melodrama, as in the murder of Mary Dalton, is sometimes very functional. At other times, it is unfortunately its own excuse for being.

And so one may go on, but when he finishes he will find *Native Son* still afloat and waiting for the next reader to make it a reference point in the fabric of his being.

Wright's vision of black men and women rendered in the four books that I have discussed stormed its way into the fabric of American culture with such fury that its threads form a reference point in the thinking and imagination of those who have yet to read him. Quickly downgraded as more art-conscious black writers made the scene, he seems now all too prophetic, and all too relevant, majestically waiting that close critical engagement which forms the greatest respect that can be paid to a great man and writer.

Thus, today, when we think that we know so much about black life, even down to its metaphysics and ambiguity, it is humbling to realize that the lifelong commitment of soul that was Richard Wright is of the essence of much that we think we know.

THE LAST TRACK
for Joe Goncalves

we sat
in the zen room
cautioned
by the heads of tribal masks
hewn from the eyes
of those who went before us/
we discussed our legacies
of custom and conduct
in white black and red metaphor
entombed
as they were
in the photos
of dead black men
our hero spirits
our Loas
deamons
      arising from gunshots
          across nations across galaxies
    the speed of light/

DAVID HENDERSON

we
    overhear
        monk
creating
new scales on western planes
obsolescent
and eternal
       it comes
       the birth of a genius
we sit
in our sundry rooms
awaiting/
       preparing

THE STEAMBOAT CAPTAIN

steamboat captain
he wear fancy clothes
and no one knows
say he's not she's not
no it's not real
————*a song by the Holy Modal Rounders*

day of skyway
looking from high terrace down on moving river
elemental american travel
emptying out into the great atlantic

railroads move on water barges
pan american helicopters bat overhead
and the low moving spiders of the police patrol
coast guard pt boats   oil company tankers   excursion boats
tugs yachts and battle ships
all move this speedway
eternal
kindred to all waterways
of america
      to move home
      and away
across the terrace
of the radical folksinger
splay the august institutions of our time
con edison atlantic gas and electric smokes away

red white and blue smokestacks
stacksmoke
     for debris of the lungs
     in hot rooms
the obsolescent brooklyn navy yard billows out along the shore
down the way brillo soap pad factory and cerveza schaefer
compete for ghetto kitchens
                look away
                look away

sunshine sammy synthesis
white women for mobility
asleep on the floor
dreaming of the efficacy of taxicabs
modern terminals of travel
train and plane jargon
of this silent white land

it might be the same city
waking up into a dream
on the smooth soft floor
with a strange woman
dressed in red
a jungle of wine bottles
and marijuana sprinkled across the rug
like mojo

a language of white powder
american pills made for synthesis
of an arbitrary metabolism
made up in the mind
laying upon the floor
for the day to come
the tape recorder in our skulls rewinds the prophecy
                     of the night before

from the herbaria
we watch the fucking moon
dip low over brooklyn
the other shore

maybe only a bennington girl
would live in a shack in mississippi
corporate strength
of the twenty percent elite
to comprehend and set
a girls school grace and etiquette

down in lands of blood and lust
those jericho songs
come from parched lips
christian soldiers trained in the marine corps
marching with flutes instead of guns
in a war without revolution.

for the commodity analysis
etched in markets in stores
co-op matches may ignite a city
or a pipe of peace
within the green room
smoke cuddles underneath short dresses
caresses warm thighs
and screams out
along the tops of distant cliffs
made sure
by the hustle of boarders
thru narrow hallways.

lay the jewish witches on the floor
make them recite ezra pound
while the electricity showers
fibers of ancient spirits
thru the contiguous rooms of america
test the intrigue fallibility of white women
the sexuality of the races
the rachel version of the bible
apocryphal old wives tales

move/ stomp
quarter to quarter
swing wide of the black ghettos
the blades and gin talkin

old testaments of the good book
from the lips of drunken men

morning/ skyaway
the sun comes bopping in
bad and ready
sol heat
thru the window the glare of snow along the river
in its season proper to its rise
we move along the lands
from room to room/
but this time he slaps her
the chorus says wail the flailing bitch
get it hot on her tongue

below the terrace
out of the ancient land a mist appears
linked by atomic weight of dead human bones
to the rock touched beneath the original city

>   *move this steamboat*
>   *big as a cliff*
>   *elemental*
>   *as the first boat*
>   *upon this river*
>   *i am the captain motherfuckers*
>   *i take no shit*
>   *and i'm not real*
>   *so be double-ware*

Travel from Home

ED BULLINS

August showers scalded our streets during the days, and the nights were without sleep from the steam and sweat. Black figures in groups crouched on each door-stoop, muttering among themselves, their eyes lit by the insect-fanned streetlights, but some pulled down long draughts from half-hidden bottles and wine jugs, and others embraced and groped, waiting for the hour before dawn when they could return to bed.

"C'mon, make dat point, mother!" Little Willy moaned.

"Can't beat you and yo prayers too, little nigger," Big Willy growled.

"Sev-vannn . . . mama . . . sev-vannn . . . haa-ahhh . . ."

Little Willy made his point.

The summer night crap game under the streetlamp was ending; the money was as tight as our tensions.

Some of us don't play, just stand on the corner under the light, ready to signal our boys when the cops cruise up, before their blue and gray pig eyes saw what they knew would be there, and before they leaped from the patrol car, scattering us into the shadows, and then picking up the coins left in the lighted circle of emptiness. And some of us only waited for the moment.

It was about three when he passed across the street in front of the billboard, head held stiffly, feet padding along like a penguin's. Eyes watched the pale stranger cross the billboard front, step into Cadence Street, no bigger than most alleys, and waddle up on the curb on the far side and pass the hollow windows of the vacant butcher shop.

"Da ho'ays, must'ta turned dat trick out early," Red said, watching him, noticing his hurried movements. He saw me check out the stranger. "Let's take him, Chuck," he said, then waiting for my move, sprang off at a lope.

I jogged behind, hearing Little Willy holler, "C'mon, mother," and tested the looseness of my legs.

He heard us and tore out in a dash. And we were after him. Red and I started pumping hard but still allowed him to keep his lead, waiting for his flabby legs to give. At the corner he turned, stretching out for the long straightaway up Thirteenth Street hill.

When we hit the corner he was a third up the block, and the incline of night street was clear before us except for the galloping figure, and I knew the race was mine.

"Turn it on, Chuck," I heard Red yell as I passed, my shirt waving behind, the blackness of night and revenge in my conked red mop.

Eyes on the doorstoops followed us, bearing down with me on the victim in that good race. The air in its summer heaviness pushed, the moist tone and taste of night in city without trees or grass was what mingled with the funk of sweat and terror. The air weighted my lung and held back his thick body. Our distance tightened like the raw lips of a wound; the far corner was a third of a block away, but I knew that I would see his blood before he reached the intersection.

He staggered, jerking his legs in a frantic effort to find control, and then he sprawled beside a trash can, his arms coming up, using the can of filth for support. I smashed my fist aside his head before he came off his knees; he rolled with some cans as they spilled across the curb; he wailed, kicking out at shadows. Red came puffing up and planted one of his long "old folks' comforts" in a kidney.

"OH LORD . . ." the stranger screamed. "OH LORD JESUS!"

"HEY, WHAT YOU BOYS DOIN'?" some older people ran from their stoops. "WHAT YOU DOIN' TO DAT WHITE MAN?" a mammy-lookin' woman said.

As the white man spun away from the soggy thumps of Red's shoes, I waited for his dribbling mouth with a chopping left hook and a straight right which split a knuckle.

"Oh Lord, Oh Lord," he whimpered on his back. "Lord God . . . have mercy on me."

We all call on Him at least once.

"ACCEPT THE SAVIOUR, THE LORD JESUS," the white missionary lady said in the skid-row rescue. The room: half-filled for the evening meal of beans and bread with coffee having a detergent tang. But we homeless and drunken had to first wait on the Lord.

"Kiss mah ass," one friend said to another, his arm about the man's bloodied head.

"What. . . ?" the bloodied man replied. "Shussck maah dick!"

"HE WILL FORGIVE YOU YOUR SINS . . . HE WILL . . ." the preacher lady continued.

"Wha don' ya come home with me, ah could hold ya in mah arms all night," the pushy one said.

"Get ya hands offa me, ya creep."

"C'mon, it ain't no sex involved . . . sex is da fardest thing from my mind. . . ." He tried to cradle the other man's bleeding head.

"JESUS . . . JESUS . . . JESUS IS . . ." the preacher lady began singing.

". . . it's just dat you's human," the drunk said.

"Shussck mah dick!" His friend pulled away.

"GODDAMMIT!" a woman screamed and hovered about them. Her short height tied her obvious muscles into a ball of biceps. "YOU BASTARDS," she said rolling up her sleeves, flexing her arms and shaking a red fist in their faces.

"Shut up! Can't decent worshipers of the Lord get some respect? . . . RESPECT!!! . . . what you're gettin', you no-good bastards!"

"Jesus . . . Jesus . . . Jesus . . ." the preacher lady crooned.

The two drunks frowned at each other and mumbled to themselves.

"JESUS . . . JESUS . . . JESUS . . ." the preacher lady raised her voice on the last chorus.

"*Respect* . . ." the muscled woman whispered the threat for the last time and sulked back to her seat.

"*Shussck our dicks,*" one of the drunks whispered, and they sat holding each other and mumbling, waiting for their beans and bread and cleansing coffee.

"He's a fag!" I heard Red tell the woman and two men as I dragged the maimed man out of the street and propped him aside a pole. The group of snoopers were drunk, or they wouldn't have interfered.

"You mean he's a queer?" one of the men asked.

"Yeah," Red said.

Sniggles rustled in the night.

"Jesus . . . I wish you'd kill the paddy mathafukker," the big woman said and turned to move away with blackness surrounding her.

One of the men followed. Soon only one shadow stood by. Seeing the remaining man, the stranger tried to twist out of my hands.

"Please . . ." he started, arms outstretched, and I sagged him with a gut punch. He vomited on my shoes.

"Mathafukker!" I kicked him in the face, feeling his teeth give.

"Don't hurt him real bad, boys," the man said from the darkness.

"We ain't . . . just showin' him a lesson, that's all," Red said.

"Damn, you guys really work over a sonna bitch, don't ya," the drunken voice said.

"We ain't gonna hurt him anymo'," Red said. "Just talk ta him and find out why he's messin' round here fo."

Then there was no one under the light but Red and me and him; he began to cry.

The poor lonely bastard.

"HEY, BOY," the bleary-eyed old man said. "Hey, boy, help me, will ya? Thank ya, son, will ya wheel me in here so I can get somethin' ta eat?

"Here's a table . . . get me a bowl of soup, will ya, and you get anything you want. . . .

"Only coffee! Hey, get yourself anything you want. Get it, I say, ya want me ta slap ya?

"Ya just got ta town? From where? . . . Oh! Been in jail! I just got out myself, ya know, kept gettin' drunk. When I got out, the only guy would help me was a colored boy, yeah, pushed me all over town . . . that boy was really okay; I bet I took him in over a dozen restaurants and the only thing he ever got was nit-nats. Yeah, just like you . . . nit-nats.

"Here's the change . . . here, take it, HERE, TAKE IT, YA. . . ! Ohhh . . . take it, fellah . . . I want ya ta have it.

"He never would eat a full meal . . . only one who helped me. . . . Hey, boy, where ya goin'! . . . Come back here when I tell ya . . . COME BACK!"

I smashed him once more in the face; his head bounced on the pavement.

"Cool it, Chuckie," Red said to me.

I turned away, breathing deep; I could feel the many

eyes back in the darkness; eyes cursing us; eyes hating us for doing the things the eyes wished to see.

Red handed me some bills in a wad; the blood from my busted hands wet them before I shoved the money into my pocket.

"Everything's straight, baby?" Red asked. I looked at him. He gave me the hit's ring; he kept the watch.

The game was over when we got back to the corner; it took close to an hour to describe the chase and the mugging.

"Yeah, I told some people he was queer and they just went bout dere business," Red repeated over and over.

"Hey, Chuck, tell us what happened on the road before you got busted and came back," Little Willy said.

"Yeah, you always makin' it somewheres, man. You's worse den some fuckkin' hobo!"

"Where you go every summer, Chuckie?" Big Willy had asked too, before the cruiser had crept up, and the cop had shouted out the window that somebody had just stomped a fag on Thirteenth Street, and that he wanted our corner and we better get our "black asses out of sight, pronto!"

"Wow, man, if he had'a searched us we'd been fucked," Red has said before we split.

"Yeah, he never thought we'd be lame enough to stand around bull shittin' bout it."

That morning as Red and I walked to our block through the early, deserted streets, me holding my aching fists, with the dawn glowing about us, Red said: "Yeah, Chuck . . . where do you go every year?"

"Man . . . it ain't far enough . . . it just ain't."

Home Is Much Too Far to Go

GEORGE DAVIS

On a sunny but cool afternoon Lewis Cooper drove toward the New England village where he had gone to college ten years before. His wife rode beside him. Their blue Oldsmobile moved comfortably along the winding country road between grassy hillsides where peaceful herds of sheep and dairy cows grazed.

The village came upon them suddenly as they rounded a curve in the road. She had never seen it before, but he had described it to her as the kind of town that you see pictured on the front of Christmas cards. It *was* that, she thought, except there was no snow on the roofs, no icicles hanging from the eaves and no snowflakes falling through the clear September air.

The elms along the streets were as fiery red as they were supposed to be in autumn in a Christmas-card New England village. The grass in the town common was beginning to die in the chill that forecast the bitter northern winter. They drove down the main street without saying anything to each other.

The business section managed to confine itself to a few small shops facing the common on the right side. Yes, she thought, it was every bit as lovely as her husband had described it, but she did not say anything. She left her husband alone with the beginnings of his memories.

He was a tall brown-skinned Negro who had gotten on well in life. God knows he had made enough money for his family of four to live comfortably.

The only regret he had about his life was that since college nothing had touched his emotions very deeply. His wife knew that he could watch a baby die and not flinch. She knew that if she were to turn to him and say, "Lewis, I want a divorce. I never want to see you again," he would simply look at her without emotion, waiting for her to make the next move.

He hated this about himself. Rather, he was mildly discontent about it, for hatred would have required more emotion than he had given anything for more than ten years. He worried about it. She worried about it too. In fact, they both agreed that it was his single big failure in an otherwise successful life.

For about a half hour they drove through some of the back sections of the town. Most of the streets were even more quiet and lovely than the main street to which they returned to take the room he had reserved at the Colonial Inn.

He wanted his wife to see the college. God knows he had told her about it often enough, but first he wanted to see it himself, alone. So he left her in the room unpacking their things.

He had come back to the village vaguely hoping to learn to feel at least something again. He had chosen not to go back to Harlem where he was born because he knew that he did not want to feel too much. He pulled the sleeves of his gray sweater midway up his forearm and started up the street toward the college. It was a small liberal-arts school which stressed close personal relationships between students and instructors and devotion to tradition, to classical languages and to classical literature. But ten years ago it had wanted to be something else. It had wanted with half its mind to be a football power, and that was how he had gotten a scholarship there.

Walking along the shady side of the common, he passed large houses with colonnaded porches. They sat in quiet dignity among the ancient trees that would have made the town almost invisible from the air. During his four years here he had never entered one of these houses. He felt a little self-conscious because when he had been a student no Negroes lived in the village. The only ones ever seen in town were the ones the school brought. But here he was, too old to be a student and too young to be a parent, moving along in the shade of the giant republican elms.

Who did the townspeople think he was, he wondered. Did they think the college had gone crazy and hired a Negro professor? These thoughts made him walk a little lighter and smile more often than he would have at the people he passed. For four years he had felt distant and detached in this fragile alien environment. But he had always been careful to smile often enough so that people did not mistake his detachment for hostility. The town had always been pleasant in its almost total disregard of his presence there for four years, especially after he quit the football team.

The entrance to the campus was at the far end of Main Street where the town square ended abruptly at the large sandstone gate donated by the class of 1907, he remembered. Beyond the gate the grass sloped upward toward the college itself, nestled on a high wooded plateau overlooking the town. Some excitement stirred in Lewis Cooper as he started up the hill.

There were no new buildings on the central campus. The last one, he remembered, had been built in 1934 out of the same golden-buff sandstone. It too was gray now and vine-covered and, like the rest, facing inward toward the central quadrangle, giving the whole campus a kind of post-Colonial, collegiate gothic unity. Even the buildings in the rear were nothing more than taller members looking over the shoulders of the others at the statue of Socrates in a circle at the intersection of the stone paths that crisscrossed the quadrangle.

He stood on the steps of the chapel and watched students going from one building to another, getting their schedules approved for the coming year's classes. It had been an all-male college when he had attended, but now there were almost as many girls as boys. There were still, he could see, only a handful of black students mixed almost invisibly with an army of white students. The white students looked about the same as the ones he had known. The hair was a little longer and the clothing a little shabbier, but nothing much had changed. He had a slight feeling of envy and dislike for them as he watched. They were still the same healthy, unmenaced children of the rich who had made his life so lonely for four years.

He did not want to go into any of the buildings where he was bound to come into contact with the students. Instead he thought of another place he could go where there would be no crowd at this time of day.

The football stadium sat in a natural bowl that made it visible as soon as he came around Longfellow Hall. Halfway down the hill he stopped at a point where the trees were thin. He could see the stands and the field from one end zone to the other. Down there, he thought, is where he had earned his ticket out of Harlem. So far it had been a ticket with no additional passengers, not even his sister or his father.

He kept on down the hill. Actually he wasn't a good football player. He was more a bookworm and a dreamer. But he was big and colored. Jim Brown was starring at Syracuse. Bo Robeson at Cornell, Johnny Counts at Illinois. The first six players on the all-American basketball team were big and colored, and there were fourteen big colored people on the 1956 Olympic Track Squad. It was a good year for athletic scholarships for big colored people, he remembered with some bitterness.

He went into the stadium and took a seat behind the south goal post. The seat was hard as he sat and looked out over the field and the other empty seats. He thought of the time as a sophomore when his sister came up to see him.

But his mind soon drifted to the drive back to New York when her visit was over.

II

By the time they reached the New York Thruway, the snow had begun falling again. A car passed and he stared at the wheels turning over in the slush. Soon he felt that one of the car's wheels had gotten stuck in the pit of his stomach and was spinning snow and grit up on his insides. Dirty water was leaking all through him. Flakes came swirling into the beams of the headlights before disappearing into the cottony darkness that surrounded them. In the car the full force of all that she had been trying to tell him hit him for the first time.

For the past four months, she said, she had not been living at home much, but had been staying down on Fiftieth Street in a hotel, selling pussy to tourists.

He was cold all over. The car mushed along. He reached forward and turned the heat up. Each time he thought of one of the things that men make whores do he felt like he was going to split wide open. He looked down at her legs, then up at her mouth.

Her face was framed by a cheap shoulder-length wig. False eyelashes jutted out about an inch from eyelids that were heavily shaded with mascara. There was a false mole stuck to the left side of her face. She was only eighteen, he thought, but she looked at least twenty-eight.

He tried to relax. She said finally, "I stayed in Boston about two days because I was afraid to come over and burden you, but then I thought that since I came this far I would be foolish not to see how you was." She smiled. "I thought I would see how you was for a minute and then get on back to the Apple."

He did not know what to say. He kept looking out at the snow. She tried to be cheerful. "I've been trying to get up to see you for a long time." Then she was silent for a while. "I wrote you a letter," she said. "I didn't mail it because it sounded so silly." She pulled a well-worn envelope from her purse. "I wrote it three months ago but didn't mail it because I didn't like the way it sounds. Ain't that silly?" She handed the letter to him.

For some reason he did not want to touch it. "You have to read it," he said.

"It sounds mushy."

"I have to keep my eyes on the road," he said.

She unfolded the paper and started to read—or since it was dark, to remember: "Dear Lew, I have been meaning to write to you for a long time now. I hope you are fine. I'm alright. Daddy is too. How is school? If you need some money write and tell me. I have a little. I think if I don't get out of the City I'm going to go crazy. I might come up to see you next Friday, if you don't mind. Can you meet me at the bus station. I read about a colored guy named Moore who plays football with you. Maybe you can get me a date with him, or a white boy for that matter (smile). Or maybe you and I can just go dancing somewhere. I bet you can't even dance being out of the City so long. Yes you can. Love, Jenny."

They were silent for a while. "What's it like?" he asked. "What?"

"You know . . . doing . . . you know."

She didn't answer immediately. "I don't know how to tell you," she said after a while. "Don't ask that, Lew."

"They treat you bad."

She shrugged. "Sometimes . . . yes . . . sometimes. Let's don't talk about that," she said.

He stared out the window and said nothing for the rest of the trip to Manhattan. As they neared home he could see that nothing had changed. The neighborhood was as dirty and threatening as he had remembered it. He thought about the kids growing up here poor and black in a country that was rich and white. He wondered at all the adjustments they would have to make to that fact. He thought about the adjustment he was going to have to make. It frightened him to think how he had narrowly missed disaster. Even now his life was still menaced.

The houses were too close to too many easy vices. Most of the people were too desperate to avoid the wine, the scag, the gambling or the dejection so close around them. Most of them would, sooner or later, let themselves fall into one of them at least once, if for no other reason than to end the nerve-racking task of tiptoeing on the brink.

They drove past Linda's apartment where he had gotten his first piece of pussy on the roof, and his second for that matter. He had screwed her every night for nearly a month before he finally wandered back to the library to spend his evenings sitting on the floor between the stacks of books.

Behind Linda's were the basketball courts and around the corner was Lucky Gorden's. He turned down 146th Street and pulled the car to a stop in front of their apartment house.

As they climbed the stair he feared that he was going back into a cage that he had narrowly escaped. Jenny unlocked all the locks on the door and pushed it open against the steel pole slanted against it. They stepped inside. The familiar odor was there—garbage was piled under the sink. A single naked light bulb glowed dimly above the small table on which he had once eaten most of his meals.

He had changed but the place was almost exactly as he had remembered it. Dirty. The same cracked plaster was hanging from the walls. As he looked the wheel inside his stomach started turning again.

His father was asleep on the sofa. Even while asleep the tension remained on the old man's face. The sofa was far too small for him and his feet were sticking straight out over the end. His face was drawn so tight that it seemed on the verge of an explosion, or he looked like one of the tendons in his neck might slash free, like a broken banjo string.

Before Lewis could take more than a few steps toward him, the old man was on his feet. His body was rigid and his mouth was hanging open. He smiled and with two great strides crossed the room and was about to embrace his son, but he stopped. He took one step backward and looked at him. His smile deepened. His hand moved up slowly and rested on the boy's shoulder. "You're looking fine," he said, "fine. If you'd called ahead I'd had something in the house for you to eat. Jenny, go down to Macklin's and get some wieners. Get something for supper. . . . How've you been, son? I seen you on TV. Looked pretty good, Mr. Lew." The old man smiled proudly.

"I'm not hungry, Daddy."

"Jenny, there's some turkey wings in the box. You can fix them." He began picking up newspapers from the floor.

The light bulb above the table was swinging as they sat and tried to talk to each other. Jenny stayed in the kitchen warming dinner. The father's voice was gruff. He was so poorly educated that he had never liked to talk to his children. When he did he was self-conscious and tense.

The son had never really known his father. The old man treated the past as if it were another life. The son knew that his father was born in Mobile and had married his mother in Birmingham and gotten her pregnant there before taking off for Detroit to find a place for them to live. He was born while his father was away. Soon they all moved to New York to live with his mother's brother. The son knew the important details of his father's life but nothing more.

The three of them ate the giant turkey wings in a stew with peas and carrots. They did not say much. After dinner Jenny went into the bedroom. Lewis followed her and stood by the window talking while she undressed. Finally he said, "I can get you a job close to school. I'll move out of the dormitory and we can get a place together until you get on your feet."

"That'd be nice," she said. She was in bed now and had to turn to look at him.

"The football coach can get you something. Fuck him. I've done enough for him. He can get you some kind of a job."

"It's cold up there, huh?"

"Not much colder than it is in New York."

"It's sure a pretty place though," she said.

The room was too familiar to him. The walls gave his words a strange empty ring. He could hear them falling into the emptiness that the snow outside made more absolute than it would have been during the summer when the windows would be up and the sound of other human voices would be coming in from the street below. He sat in the large chair talking to her until she fell asleep.

Their mother had died in this room when he was only twelve. She had been ill for a long time but had put off going to the doctor's because she complained that doctors never told her anything that she did not know already. He remembered her lying on the bed with something bleeding inside her; she was rolling over and screaming for someone to help her.

He called the hospital, but the attendant kept asking if he was sure that she hadn't taken an overdose. He told the man that his mother never used whiskey, much less heroin, but the man seemed not to believe him. Blood came out of her mouth and she reached out to grab someone's hand, but both he and his sister had moved back, afraid. She reached out again, but there was nothing either of them could do. The ambulance came after she was dead. A trickle of blood was still moving down the side of her face.

He did not sleep well in the big chair. When he woke up he found himself lying across the bed where his sister had been. He got up and went to the other room where his father stood looking out the window. The snow had stopped.

"Where's Jenny? Good morning. Where's Jenny?" he asked.

"She'll be back before long," the father said. He did not turn from the window. He began to talk about her trouble. He said that he didn't know she was doing it until she had been at it for about two months. He said he threatened to kill her, but she simply moved away from home.

"Last night was the first time I seen her in I don't know how long," he said. He did not turn from the window. He began complaining about his job and the way the people he worked for thought he was a fool or a slave. He complained about the neighborhood which, he knew, was no place to bring up children. "A man's got to do the best he can though," he said.

"Did Jenny tell you I was taking her with me?" the son said.

"She mentioned it." The old man turned around now. "She told me to tell you though to go on without her. She said she didn't want to be dragging you down."

"Bullshit, where is she?"

"I don't know." He stared at his son for a long time. "She could be in Baltimore, Rochester, anywhere by now. I looked for her a month once and couldn't find her. But I'm going to stop her from doing what she's been doing, if that's what you worried about. I'm gon' use my fist on her, that's what I'm gon' start doing," he said hopelessly.

"I can get her a job, Daddy."

"She's pregnant, Lewis."

They did not take their eyes off one another.

"She's pregnant and she said she wants to be by herself. She goin' on and havin' this love baby, she said, so she can go ahead and fix it so she can't have any more."

That had all happened in what seemed like another life too. Students started pouring into the stadium. Lewis Cooper left to go back to the inn to bring his wife up to see the school.

She was at the mirror brushing her hair when he came into the room. "I'll be ready in a minute," she said.

He took off his sweater and put on a sports coat.

"While we're back east why don't we drive to New York so you can see your folks?" She was tall and thin and her blond hair reached to her shoulders.

"We don't have time," he said.

"Oh, sure, we could. We can afford to get back to Tacoma a day late," she pleaded.

"No," he said. She knew by his tone not to try and push him.

CAROLE CLEMMONS

MIGRATION

She stood hanging wash before sun
and occasionally watched the kids
gather acorns from the trees,
and when her husband came,
complaining about the tobacco spit on him
they decided to run North.
for a free evening.
She stood hanging wash in the basement
and saw the kids sneak puffs from cigarettes,
fix steel traps with cheese
and when her husband came,
complaining of the mill's drudgery,
                    she burst—
said he had no hunter's heart
beat him with a broom,
became blinded by the orange sun
racing into steel mill flames
and afterwards,
sat singing spirituals to sons.

NINA SIMONE

Curved back now
from the notes, the microphone and us,
she played and replayed my fate.
Grand pianoed,
bitch black she sat in gold
and with her fingers and woolsong
gave us the blues—
those blues deep in all of us,
that aches and waits for the drink and a night out to
                                  stalk itself.

LOVE FROM MY FATHER

Left like water in glasses overnight
in a cold house,
iced children are fierce.
They see fathers slobbering, staggering
into the living room chair
and race through his pockets for nickels and quarters.
The cold gives the children pneumonia and sends
red balloons tied to hospital beds, and
a caseworker to turn the heat on.
There are many gifts,
other drunks sleep in thrown paper
and green wine bottles behind billboards
but my father brings fresh glazed donuts in a white bag.

UNTITLED

If we could eat
past lynchings,
and live from the labor
that broke so many slaves,
black artists could move
        through ghettoes
like grandma grew greens in her garden.

I'M JUST A STRANGER HERE
HEAVEN IS MY HOME

The first sign was your hair
unstraightened, shortened from worry,
and it had only been a year since the wedding,
but you had grown older, Mama.
I felt your usual care
in the mustard greens, sweet potatoes and chicken,
yet you smelled of whiskey and prayer.
I showed you the pictures,
asked which you'd like remade
and watched you fidget, unable to see them.
Raising your arm, you spoke of your rheumatism,
it seems life left your arm first,
like crumbs given to frontyard robins.
Age and need, those simple weeds,
were gathering around and taking you away.

Cold Ben,
New Castle

They could see them from the gully. They also could see—could see them from the hill. In other words, they (hunters) could see them (lions), and they (lions) could see them (hunters).

Not knowing if the others had seen them, no one moved. If they moved from atop the mountain ledge, they below might think that they had been spotted. And if they thought they had been spotted, they would aim and fire right off rather than lose the killing—or their lives.

Also, if they moved, if they just flinched their fingers (the sweating oiled the triggers of the rifles, the nozzles pointed down), or if they moved their free hands to tip their hats (the sun was high, it being near noon on the left side), or if their jaws crunched on the tobacco too vigorously, they knew that they on the mountain would take off—somewhere.

It was four for four. Below, four hunters, booted, kerchiefs hugging their necks, khaki pants starched; above, four tan-yellow cats on their haunches, resting on a ledge of the triangular hill, forelegs straight, their ears pricked, their whiskers glinting in the sun.

BARRY BECKHAM

One of them, Ben, calculated fifty, seventy-five yards. Look at how they sit up there, he thought—sitting up there like four purring pussies. He was about to lick his lips but caught himself, and his heart did a two-step at the possibility that he had almost blown the whole thing. Must be over two hundred, he thought, all of them, although he couldn't make out the size of one who was too far back, it still had a head as large as the other three.

If they jumped from the ledge into the narrow gully— suddenly Ben sensed the gully surrounding them was un- usually, exceptionally narrow—if they did that, what could the four below do? Those paws, he knew, and knew they all knew, although there could be no conversation now, for it would all have to be by instinct—those paws concealed six inches of claws. Those claws could work reverse surgery on a face.

And neither could communicate. Well, actually, those below couldn't. But they knew that the others could, probably were, probably had been since they had come into the gully. They were probably talking their animal talk, planning, and with this, Ben decided, of course they see us, of course! They're just waiting for us to make our move, that's all. But then he convinced himself that they had come into the gully before they had taken the ledge. Or had they taken the ledge before they had wandered into the gully? These were important differences, for if they had walked in first, then possibly they had not been spotted. But if they had walked into the gully after they had squatted, then surely they must have seen them enter. That's what he had thought, that's what bothered Ben, and he was certain that it was bothering the other three hunters. Or were they aware of these subtleties?

Something else bothered him as a cloud darkened his (and he was sure theirs too) sight and they were silhouetted up there on the ledge for an instant, blending into the cliffs. Why didn't they either run, slide down the other side of the ledge, or why didn't they jump them if they had come first and hence knew they were in the gully? And even if they had not come first, they must have known they were in the gully, so why did they crouch up there like stuffed animals in a shooting gallery? Tense for the jump? Ignoring them? Waiting for them to move first? Plain arrogance?

If they jumped. Now, if they jumped, there would be four of these ferocious, six-inched claws coming down on them. Two hundred pounds. How would they know which to shoot? Suppose each of them shot at the same one, whereby three would be free to fall upon them. They couldn't make assignments now—"You take the one on the far left," and so forth—because speech was now taboo. They couldn't turn their heads to motion to one another either. They could not move.

Did the others realize their predicament? Ben wondered if they realized. It was he who had brought them here, had given them a piece of the action. Suppose some dummy decided to take out a handkerchief and blow his nose? He didn't even know them all, which was a handicap, for if he did, then he could feel more comfortable, could feel that they, through a long-lasting fellowship, would understand they were in a possible bear garden of confusion. He had little familiarity with them, little control over them, little sympathy for them.

Ben had just happened to be in the lodge, had been enjoying Gene Autry on the jukebox while drinking sweet green Coors and losing at poker with these guys around the table when one of them, tottering from the brew (suppose he was high?), the brim of his ten-gallon hat resting in the middle of his head, said, "Anybody for lion huntin'?" And they were out the door.

Plus, one of them is black, he thought. No telling what that nigger might do in a jam; no reason at all for him to want to help us, no reason whatsoever. And I know nothing about their kind any way. Definitely cannot count on him. So what did he have here? One guy probably high (he wished he could turn to look at the man's eyes), a nigger, and one other who appeared to Ben to be over fifty.

And they were still up there and—and one moved! One came to the edge of the ledge, stood there on all fours (the four watching him), yawned, (tongue as big as my hand, he thought), looked down. A breeze blew Ben's kerchief to his lips. If they shot at him, would the others run or jump? They saw them, they knew they were down there. Who would make the first move? Even when they jumped—he was certain they would now, anytime that big one got up and looked down on them like that, they were going to jump—they would have only one shot each. Four shots. Had to be in the head. The other three were still squatting. The other three were still standing. Of the four shots, Ben thought he might be able to count on one, his own, since the nigger—who ever heard of a Negro hunting for lions?—would panic, the drunken one would miss and the old man would faint. One for four. All for one, or one for all. A four flush hand. He was definitely working with the wrong people, the wrong characters.

I'm sorry, very very sorry I have gotten involved in this shit, thought Ben. There were some good possibilities when we first came into the gully, but I just wasn't aware of what I had to work with, what the real possibilities were. I thought I had some real characters who would see me through this difficulty, but no. Had I been smart, I would have just taken off by myself, or I should have let them walk me up the stretch past the plain and then wave goodbye and let them see me off. I should have seen to it that they were believable hunters, but who will believe that I went out with a nigger, an old man and a drunk? Now, assuming things will go along as they usually do, the lions will jump, we will shoot and something will have happened. But nothing has happened. Nothing seems to be about to happen. I don't think the lions will jump first; they usually don't. This is not the usual way. Should something happen? Of course, otherwise it would be ridiculous, we would be standing here all night. But has it been an interesting experience? Yes, it has been, he decided, and scary as hell too. Why does something have to happen? Because it usually does, we're used to it. If nothing happened, it would be an inconvenience, we'd be stuck here. Yet, if something does happen, it will be bad for us, it could really be the end, and if I had considered that possibility, I would never have started this shit.

Should I make something happen or not, he thought. It would be rather easy, it would end the long wait for us, I could just aim and shoot. But then it would be all over. If something happens, it would be the end of things for today. But that is the way these matters are handled. If I don't shoot, this inactivity continues inactively; if I shoot, it's all over. A good pun there, he reasoned. I should have thought, *when* I shoot, it's all over.

Suppose I just stop considering this shit and let the others worry about it, Ben suggested to himself. Suppose I just forget about the whole thing, just fade out. I've done my part, haven't I? I introduced these bums, brought them to a situation, caused emotional juices to flow. What more? I shouldn't have to do things as they're always done. This is enough. The hell with it.

Race and Revolution

Hexagram 49—Fire and Water

JULIUS LESTER

TEXT. *Revolution. Not before the day of its completion will we have faith in it—sublime success! Determination in a righteous course brings reward; regret vanishes.*

COMMENTARY. *In this hexagram, water and fire extinguish each other, behaving like two women who live together but whose wills conflict—such is the nature of revolution. That faith is not reposed in it until the day of its completion means that revolution must come first, whereafter public faith in it will be established. A civilized and enlightened attitude brings joy; great success makes it possible to put all things to rights. Upon the achievement of a necessary revolution, regret vanishes. The renovating activities of the celestial and terrestrial forces produce the progress of the four seasons.*

———I Ching   *Translated by John Blofield*
       (*Dutton, 1968*)

Let us not talk falsely now
The hour is getting late.

————Bob Dylan

Whether or not the revolutionary possibilities that exist
in this country are fulfilled depends, in great part, on
whether black and white youth (upon whom the responsi-
bility for making a revolution mainly falls) can understand
each other. At present, the prospect is uncertain. White youths
are just becoming aware of their own racism and this awareness has not yet led them to the means for destroying it.
Even the best of white youth (the long-hairs) manifest racism on myriad levels, some of which they are able to recognize; others of which they are not. Black youths have
broken off communications with whites, which is under-
standable, justifiable and long overdue. To put it differently
and more accurately, black youths are limiting themselves
to communicating only with each other. Yet, this process has
resulted in sudden blind spots in the black mind to what
has been and is now transpiring among white youth. Indeed,
the "long-hairs" are subjected to as much scorn from blacks as
from George Wallace. One of the great ironies is to hear a
daishiki-clad, Afro-coiffed black refer to hippies with the
same hostility and language used by a lower-class white. It
is not only ironic; it may be a fatal mistake.

What happened among white youths in the sixties and
continues into the seventies (at least thus far) is one of
the most remarkable occurrences in American history. The
white sons and daughters of middle-class America demanded its death. Blacks have looked upon these white
youths with a great deal of skepticism, as well they might.
It is exceedingly difficult to trust any white person, even a
white person one might love.

(Many times I've heard young blacks remark, "How can
I trust some dirty, filthy hippie? Hell, he take a bath and get
a haircut and he's white again. Right? Me, I'm gon' be black
from now until. I ain't gon' cop out when the shit gets
rough." But the revolutionary commitment of a black is a
matter of necessity; blacks have no choice in the matter—
whites do. Thus, the white who chooses to cut his hair and

go home is exercising one choice available to him. How many blacks would not also exercise the choice if they had it? Blacks cannot cop out simply because white America won't let them. Thus, they shouldn't be so self-righteous about their commitment.)

For every white who has chosen to go back home, there is another who has left home. Where blacks are condemned to fight because of the color of their skin, white youth recognized in the sixties that they were condemned to fight by virtue of who they were—America's golden children, the most affluent, educated generation in the history of the country. But their own experiences in this society led them to hate it just as the experience of blacks had led them to hate it. The specifics of their experiences have been vastly different; yet, each is not a whole unto itself, but merely part of a mosaic.

Blacks too often feel that their experience is the only valid one. "You can never know what it's like to be black," they scream, and it is an unchallengeable truth. Conversely, the black youth can never know what it is like to grow up in Manhasset, Scarsdale, Pasadena, Rockland, or any of the other concentration camps from which white youths are escaping. Black youths, in their anger at whites, seek to invalidate any experience of whites, just as whites, for so many centuries, failed to recognize the validity of the black experience. (Not too many yet recognize it.) But the white youth's cultural revolution and the black revolution of the sixties were different manifestations of the same thing: the beginnings of a definitive break with Western civilization.

It is ironic that at the very moment when blacks reached the point of letting out their hundreds of years of rage, young whites, in part because of blacks, reached a point of recognizing that they were being prepared to be the beneficiaries of all the evil forces of the modern world. They said NO to what was in their line of vision; blacks said NO to what was in their line of vision. Tragically, they could not also see what the other saw. Yet, at the same time the young hippie was catching hell from his parents for his shoulder length hair, the young black nationalist was catching hell from his parents for his Afro. At the same time the young hippie was being scorned by his parents for his beaded head-band, or the young hippie girl for her mini-skirt, the young black was being threatened by his parents for wearing a daishiki. The parents of the young black told him, "Studying Swahili won't get you a good job. You talkin' about Black Power and ain't got sense enough to realize you need some Green Power." And the parent of the young white shouted, "Turn that stereo down! Bob Dylan's not going to pass your college boards for you. The Beatles aren't going to give you a job. You won't even be able to get a job because your ear-drums will have been shattered by that horrible music."

They were brother and sister, the young black militant and white hippie, fighting different faces of the American Nightmare. They were brother and sister, seeking to rede-fine their lives within the limits of their own experiences. And for once, young whites were more aware of blacks than blacks of whites. Blacks, by necessity, have always had to know white America better than it knew itself. But the ne-cessity of knowing one's black self in the sixties resulted in a myopia regarding the events taking place inside white America. At the very instant when white America ceased to be a unity, at the very moment the house divided against itself, the vision of blacks became blurred.

White youth, on the other hand, were very much aware of blacks. Indeed, whites have always been aware of blacks, because they sought spiritual sustenance from black culture since the first black singer flatted a third. Whites have tried to sing as blacks do, play jazz as blacks do, talk as blacks do, and dress as blacks do. And at the same time, whites have exploited the culture for profit, as well as tried to deny that it had any validity. (See Le Roi Jones's *Blues People*: *Negro Music in White America* for further details.)

The white youth of the sixties began as imitators of black culture. They started with the rural Southern blues and moved to the 1940's urban blues of Chicago. If it had ended there, it would have meant little, except once again, whites were playing at being black and making fools of themselves. (What is more silly than a white boy from

Westchester County playing a guitar and singing, "I ain't gon' plow no cotton, I ain't gon' hoe no corn." You goddam right!)

Fortunately, it did not end there. The Rolling Stones took their name from a song of Muddy Waters. The Beatles began as imitators of Chuck Berry and Muddy Waters. Bob Dylan had his roots deep in the music of the rural blues. But the Stones, the Beatles, Dylan and practically all the rest stopped trying to use the words of black songs to express their own experiences and began speaking directly from their lives. Those white musicians who were to become the voices of the new generation of white youth had been shaped and molded by different forces than any previous generation. They were the children upon whom the dust of Hiroshima had settled, and it had made a qualitative difference in the way they viewed themselves and their country. Instead of ending as mere imitators of black culture, they used that culture as a springboard toward the creation of their own means of expression.

Writing in 1957, Norman Mailer recognized that something was happening in America and he discussed it in one of the most brilliant and prophetic essays of the twentieth century, "The White Negro." Mailer recognized a new social type in the personage of a figure he called "the Hipster." In his description of "the Hipster" he defined the world that young whites were then facing, the world to which they would react by becoming hipsters in 1957 and hippies in 1966:

> . . . the hipster, the man who knows that if our collective condition is to live with instant death by atomic war . . . or with a slow death by conformity with every creative and rebellious instinct stifled . . . then the only life-giving answer is to accept the terms of death, to live with death as immediate danger, to divorce oneself from society, to exist without roots, to set out on that uncharted journey into the rebellious imperatives of the self. . . . One is Hip or one is Square . . . trapped in the totalitarian tissues of American society, doomed willy-nilly to conform if one is to succeed.

The only sector of society that the hipster could regard as a model was black society, for blacks had "been living on the margin between totalitarianism and democracy for two centuries." They lived continually in the shadow of death and this forced them to approach America with a totally different set of attitudes, attitudes that whites began to learn as they found themselves more and more alienated from America. Blacks knew that "life was war, nothing but war," and this knowledge led to what Mailer calls "the art of the primitive."

> He [the black man] believed in the enormous present, he subsisted for his Saturday night kicks, relinquishing the pleasures of the mind for the more obligatory pleasures of the body, and in his music he gave voice to the character and quality of his existence, to his rage and the infinite variations of joy, lust, languor, growl, cramp, pinch, scream and despair of his orgasm.

The above has become one of the most controversial passages in "The White Negro." Mailer's critics have accused him of giving legitimacy to racist stereotypes of blacks, of paternalistic racism, of seeing blacks as nothing more than "partying, balling fools." Mailer's description does leave something to be desired. (Blacks never "relinquished the pleasures of the mind" as much as these "pleasures" were never made available to them.) Yet, despite the failure of Mailer's language to convey all that he means, what he is saying is of the utmost importance. W. E. B. Du Bois said it in 1897 in his essay, "The Conservation of Races." Du Bois argued that it was the obligation of blacks to retain their racial identity because it was through race that groups of people made their unique contributions to the world. Blacks "are that people whose subtle sense of song has given America its only American music, its only American fairy tales, its only touch of pathos and humor amid its mad money-getting plutocracy." If Du Bois had been raised in an environment where black culture was more evident, rather than in New England, he would have been able to elucidate even further. But, that more detailed explication comes in the twentieth century in the writings of Léopold Senghor, the father of negritude.

Negritude is the whole of the value of civilization—cultural, economic, social, political—which characterize the black peoples. . . . It is essentially *instinctive reason*, which pervades all these values. It is reason of the impressions, reason that is "seized." It is expressed by the emotions through an abandonment of self and a complete identification with the object; through the myth of the archetype of the collective soul, and the *myth primordial* accorded to the cosmos. In other terms, the sense of communion, the gift of imagination, the gift of rhythm—these are the traits of Negritude, that we find like an indelible seal on all the works and activities of the black man.
(From *Léopold Sédar Senghor and the Politics of Negritude* by Irving Leonard Markovitz, p. 41.)

The spiritual means that whites have used to exist in this world have been inadequate and have, in fact, brought the world close to extinction. (I know it is difficult for whites to admit that they have fucked up humanity like no one else could ever have dreamed, but, please, "Let's not talk falsely now. The hour is getting late.") Western civilization has been characterized by reason, by rational thought. And reason has been applied in every facet of human existence, from making a plate to organizing society. Reason, however, is the most limited of man's faculties. It is fine for solving a mathematical problem, or for building a bridge. But when it takes precedence over all the other faculties of man, it can only be destructive. Unchecked reason builds atomic bombs, develops germ warfare, drops napalm and tolerates poverty and slums. It is not that man's moral and spiritual sensibilities are underdeveloped; they have merely been tyrannized by the glorification of reason. "I think; therefore I am," said Descartes. How sick can you get? Senghor has brilliantly etched the Western malady in *Senghor: Prose and Poetry*:

Let us consider first the European as he faces an object. He is . . . an objective intelligence, a man of will, a warrior, a bird of prey, a steady gaze. He first distinguishes the object from himself. He keeps it at a distance. He freezes it out of time and, in a way, out of space. He fixes it, he kills it. With his precision instruments he dissects it in a pitiless factual analysis. As a scientist, yet at the same time prompted by practical considerations, the European makes use of the *Other* that he has killed in this way for his practical ends. He makes a *means* of it. With a centripetal movement he assimilates it. He destroys it by devouring it. "White men are cannibals," an old sage from my own country told me a few years ago. "They have no respect for life." It is this process of devouring which they call "humanizing nature" or more exactly "domesticating nature." "But," went on the old sage . . . "what they don't take into account, these whites, is that life cannot be domesticated, nor especially can God who is the source of all life, in whom all life shares. . . . It is life which makes human, not death. I am afraid that it may all turn out very badly. The whites by their madness to destroy will in the end bring down troubles upon us."

And it is this fact about the West that young whites became increasingly aware of as they found themselves choking from the lack of humanity in their immediate environments. "I try my best/To be just like I am/But everybody wants you/To be just like them," was one of Bob Dylan's definitions of what he had to confront. And he concluded simply, "I ain't gonna work on Maggie's farm no more."

Being young and white in America became a frightening experience as it was realized that they were supposed to inherit the lives of people who, as Dylan put it, "despise their jobs, their destinies" and "Cultivate their flowers to be/ Nothing more than something/They invest in."

There had to be an alternative and young whites found it in a black culture in which they immersed themselves more and more. They, like Mailer's hipster, were "trying to create a new nervous system for themselves."

. . . we . . . act with a nervous system which has been formed from infancy, which carries in the style of its circuits the very contradictions of our parents and our early milieu . . . we are obliged . . . to meet the tempo of the present and the future with reflexes and rhythms which come from the past. It is not only the "dead weight of the institutions of the past" but indeed the inefficient . . . antiquated nervous circuits of the past which strangle our potentiality for responding to new possibilities . . .

Writing when he did, it was, of course, impossible for Mailer to know exactly how the situation would evolve. The hipster of the fifties was, in Mailer's term, a "psychopath," a criminal, who was seeking to break the stranglehold of Western civilization in acts of violence. The duck-tailed, hot-rodding juvenile delinquent of the fifties who listened to Elvis Presley and Bill Haley and the Comets (as well as the middle-class white kids who did not adopt the style of the j.d.'s) were the forerunners of the long-haired, marijuana-smoking hippie of the sixties listening to the Jefferson Airplane. The other variant on the hipster was the Beat Generation, which Mailer characterizes as simply another manifestation of the bohemian artist. They were more than that, however, for, unlike the bohemian artist of the past, the Beat Generation was not rebelling against Western civilization as much as it was working its way toward something new—an alternate culture. The Beat Generation was born in the reaction to the world view of the hipster quoted earlier.

The sixties is the coming together of the two "antisocial," i.e., anti-American, anti-Western tendencies of the fifties—the hipster and the Beat Generation. These two joined with an entirely new force in the sixties—the political rebellion of blacks. The hipsters ceased to be self-destructive psychopaths unable to find "some way out of here" (James Dean) and became the most religious generation in this country's history. They didn't want to worship God. They wanted to be God. Not the God who ruled, but the God who loved.

The catalytic force in this transformation of white youths from psychopathic hipsters and beatniks was the civil rights movement, which Mailer predicted.

. . . the organic growth of Hip depends on whether the Negro emerges as a dominating force in American life. Since the Negro knows more about the ugliness and danger of life than the white, it is probable that if the Negro can win his equality, he will possess a potential superiority, a superiority so feared that the fear itself has become the underground drama of domestic politics . . . the Negro's equality would tear a profound shift into the psychology, the sexuality, and the moral imagination of every white alive.

Mailer erred only in basing his prediction on blacks winning "equality." This assumes that by "equality" he meant equality of political, social and economic opportunities and rights under the law. It was the attempt by blacks to achieve this equality that thrust them into the superior position in the minds of young whites, for blacks had moral rightness. There was no question about it. Indeed, blacks became the cutting edge, the standard by which young whites measured themselves. By their mere existence, blacks were the moral conscience of America. In the sixties, a significant portion of white American youth responded to that fact.

Mailer concludes his prognosis on the evolution of hip with an astoundingly accurate prediction, one which describes the sixties and takes us into the seventies:

With this possible emergence of the Negro, Hip may erupt as a psychically armed rebellion whose sexual rhythm may rebound against the antisexual foundation of every organized power in America, and bring into the air such animosities, antipathies, and new conflicts of interest that the mean empty hypocrisies of mass conformity will no longer work. A time of violence, new hysteria, confusion and rebellion will then be likely to replace the time of conformity. At that time, if the liberal should prove realistic in his belief that there is peaceful room for every tendency in American life, then Hip would end by being absorbed as a colorful figure in the tapestry. But if this is not the reality, and the economic, the social, the psychological and finally the moral crises accompanying the rise of the Negro should prove insupportable, then a time is coming when every political guidepost will be gone, and millions of liberals will be faced with political dilemmas they have so far succeeded in evading, and with a view of human nature they do not wish to accept. . . . What the liberal cannot bear to admit is the hatred beneath the skin of a society so unjust that the amount of collective violence buried in the people is perhaps incapable of being contained, and therefore if one wants a better world one does well to hold one's breath, for a worse world is bound to come first, and the dilemma may well be this: given such hatred, it must either vent itself nihilistically or become turned into the cold murderous liquidations of the totalitarian state.

Whether the hatred of which Mailer speaks will "vent itself nihilistically" or in the form of a "totalitarian state" is the question of the hour.

2

. . . theories don't explain us—
a revolutionary movement that has
come out of affluence, not poverty. . . .
We are exploited and oppressed, and
we are fighting for our freedom.
Capitalism will die because it cannot
satisfy its own children!

——Jerry Rubin

The white youth of the sixties had a difficult and painful job, a job that was more painful to do than that required by blacks. For white youth had to completely disassociate themselves from their own people. Black youth merely had to come together with their own. Black youth could look at their parents and at least know that they had tried, against overwhelming odds, that they had done what they thought was right with their limited resources. White youths looked at their parents and saw moral cretins, saw people who had raised them to believe that "Negroes are as good as anybody else" until their daughter walked in the door with one. (One father of an acquaintance of mine called his daughter a "nigger-fucker," beat her up and called the police to have her committed, all because she was a supporter of the Black Panther Party. She was thirty and the mother of two.) Blacks could not really appreciate the suffering of young whites. It was not clothed in rats and roaches and cold winter winds. No, it came in $35,000 homes, cars, money to spend, fashionable clothes, the best education. So how, blacks wanted to know, could they be suffering? Easy. Man does not live by bread alone, and the white youth of the sixties could feel it in the loneliness of bedrooms which were as large as tenement apartments. Sandy Darlington described their plight in the *San Francisco Express Times*:

So many of us were dealt a mortal wound at a tender age. When we left home, dad and mom said good-bye at the door, and gave us a good-luck pat on the back as we went. But it wasn't a pat, it was a hatchet sinking chunk deep into our backs: there, you little prick, you thought you'd get away from us, eh? Like the ending of a gangster flick, you win everything except your life.

And so we stagger out into the world, into life, with this Thing stuck in our back, festering, killing us by inches, and we only have a few years to squirm until that weapon works its way out or destroys us.

They found that the only way they could begin to work that weapon out of their backs was through exposure to and immersion in black culture. Janis Joplin started imitating Bessie Smith records (and still hasn't stopped) and she learned that when she did so "she experienced a thrilling sense of release." Hundreds of thousands of others found the same when they listened to black blues singers or the white imitators. Black music, even watered down by white blues singers, released them from the prison of those selves bequeathed to them by their parents. But what is it about black music, indeed blacks as a whole, that has this remarkable power to subvert an ever-increasing number of whites from the American way? Some call it Soul; others simply call it "style." Even the poorest, downest brother or sister has a certain style, a certain way of walking, talking and just being . . . even when starving to death. Senghor defines it as "the African apprehension of reality," which he contrasts with the European approach to the world discussed previously. Where whites have separated themselves from nature and each other, the African (and his brothers and sisters in involuntary exile) has not. Even in the United States, blacks are closer to Senghor's definition (from *Senghor: Prose and*

Poetry) of an African relationship to the world than to a European one.

> The African . . . does not begin by distinguishing himself from the object, the tree or stone, the man or animal or social event. He does not keep it at a distance. He does not analyze it. Once he has come under its influence, he takes it like a blind man, still living, into his hands. He does not fix it or kill it. He turns it over and over in his supple hands, he fingers it, he *feels* it. . . . He is *moved* to his bowels, going out in a centrifugal movement from the subject to the object on the waves sent out from the *Other* . . . the Negro . . . reacts more faithfully to the stimulus of the object. He is wedded to its rhythm. This physical sense of rhythm, rhythm of movements, forms and colors, is one of his specific characteristics, for rhythm is the essence of energy itself. It is rhythm which is at the basis of imitation and which plays a determining role in man's generic activity and in his creative activity: in memory, language and art.

The black is much more ready to relinquish his ego "his I . . . and identify himself with the THOU." (See the chapter on Cultural Nationalism in this writer's *Look Out, Whitey! Black Power's Gon' Get Your Mama!* for a detailed discussion of this phenomenon in black culture.) "He dies to himself to be reborn in the *Other*. He does not assimilate. He is assimilated. He does not kill the other life, he strengthens his own life through it."

Through black music, the African apprehension of reality was opened a little to whites. (Through drugs, it was opened even more.) The music took the young whites out of themselves and, for the first time in their lives, they FELT. Those who were directly involved in the civil rights movement and social work projects with blacks, those who had close personal relationships with blacks, were exposed even more to the African apprehension of reality. Through blackness, drugs, Oriental religions and philosophies, young whites learned the truth of Senghor's assertion: "Classical European reason is analytical and makes use of the object. African reason is intuitive and participates in the object." They felt in their guts that it was far superior to be a participant than a user. Indeed, their parents had used them, not participated in them.

When whites began imitating black music, blacks were naturally insulted, feeling that once again whites were coming to steal and to make money off their culture. There was also no little feeling of hurt on the part of blacks that they could never have anything for themselves without whites wanting in on it. (My own rage at this "encroachment" upon what is mine still exists, even though I now understand what it is young whites are trying to get at. Yet, so often, in their attempts to get at it, they display their racism. For example, whites quickly picked up on the expression "Right on!" and used it with pride, as if it were their own. I and many blacks resented it. "Get your own muthafucking expression, white boy. Goddam! Can't you even talk for yourself?) But, with the creation of rock, it became clear that just as blacks had taken Western music, adapted it to their needs, passed it through the African filter and created something new, whites were now taking black music and passing it through their own existences and, for the first time, white music became a weapon against America.

The sound of it was loud, penetrating, even painful. It was an approximation of emotion to be apprehended not by the ear, but by the gut. (In *Prose and Poetry* Senghor says that not only music is apprehended with the body, but games, too.

> . . . games reproduce the natural gestures of man and African music and dancing, which are closely related to each other as indeed are all music and dancing, reproduce the movements of the human body, which is itself in harmony with the movements of the brain and of the world: the beating of the heart, breathing, the rhythm of walking and making love, ebb and flow, succession of days and seasons and, in general, all the rhythms of the cosmos.)

The new music of the young whites was not a music to be merely listened to, not unless one listened with his entire being (which is the way one should listen to Bach, Beethoven, Brahms and any of the great classical composers.

Unfortunately, the West called them artists and shoved them into music appreciation courses where they are dissected and appreciated and never experienced). One cannot experience anything if the brain has out its tentacles, analyzing, verbalizing and, just generally getting in the way. Senghor explains the African apprehension of reality in physiological terms.

> . . . the rhythm of the object is transmitted to the subject through the nerve cells, so that at the height of the emotion the rhythms of the heart and the breath fall into agreement with it, as for example, in music and dancing. It has been noticed that the rhythms of movement . . . dancing and music . . . [ellipses in original] probably because they are more closely related to the physiological rhythms, are those least transformed by the brain which here plays no more than the part of a relay station as it were. One of my friends, an African poet, confessed to me that all forms of beauty strike him at the root of the belly and give rise to a sexual feeling. This not only with music, dancing or an African mask, but with a painting by Giotto or a Florentine palace. It goes even further, for the symbolic imagery, visual as well as auditory, of a High Mass has the same effect on him. Someone will raise the cry of eroticism. It would be more accurate to talk of sensuality. But the African's spirituality is rooted in his sensuality: in his physiology.

It was toward this end that the white youth culture was moving. It was no accident that seminudity became the norm for the young. Bras were discarded as being what they were—blasphemers of the female body. Attitudes toward sex changed among the white youth culture and fucking ceased to be the disgusting act of animals but the most beautiful thing any two (three or four) people could do with each other. Men's and women's clothes exploded in the colors of the sun and spoke of LIFE LIFE LIFE and it was worth being alive merely to look at the clothes people wore.

No, the young whites of the sixties were not trying to be black. They were "trying to save their souls," as Albert Goldman so strikingly put it. "Adopting as a tentative identity the firmly set, powerfully expressive mask of the black man, the confused, conflicted and frequently self-doubting and self-loathing offspring of Mr. and Mrs. America are released into an emotional and spiritual freedom denied them by their own inherited culture." To put it differently, who can really blame white youth for trying not to be white? They should be complimented.

American society was in trouble, deep trouble. Its youth were not only rejecting it, but trying to kill it. "We are not protesting 'issues,'" said Jerry Rubin. "We are protesting Western civilization." Abbie Hoffman said what Mailer had been afraid to put so bluntly: "We are niggers." The politics of the youth culture was not a politics of the head; it was a politics of Being, "a politics of the nervous system," said Timothy Leary, a phrase of which Senghor would undoubtedly approve. "Our politics is our music, our smell, our skin, our hair, our warm naked bodies, our drugs, our energy, our underground papers, our vision," Rubin declared.

Previous generations of Americans had been alienated from Western civilization, and literature and art are filled with their pain and despair over the matter. This generation *alienated itself* from Western civilization and was ecstatic about it. The quicker, the better. "I'd rather have my country die for me," sang the Jefferson Airplane nonchalantly. And Dylan told his contemporaries to "Leave your stepping stones behind" and "Strike another match, go start anew/ And it's all over now, baby blue."

The young whites could not identify with blacks. Learn from them, yes. Be like them, no. They had to be themselves and that was the road they traveled in the sixties and they succeeded in recreating themselves. They identified with each other and against "them" who, as the Jefferson Airplane sang, "In loyalty to their kind/They cannot tolerate our minds/And in loyalty to our kind/We cannot tolerate their obstruction." They set themselves in opposition to those they were supposed to follow and looked at each other and realized, in the words of the Beatles, that "I am he as you are he as you are me and we are all together." And the Jefferson Airplane went even further and identified themselves as "outlaws in the eyes of America" who were "obscene lawless hideous dangerous dirty violent and young." And they were proud, boasting that "We are forces of chaos and anarchy/Everything they say we are we are."

Yet, blacks remain unconvinced, which is not surprising. Indeed, while the white youth culture does have its roots, to a certain extent, in black culture, white youth culture is going in contrary motion to the road a lot of blacks are traveling. While the white young are trying to get away from as much of Western civilization as they can—cities, prepackaged and frozen foods, housing that more and more resembles coffins—many blacks would like some of the economic advantages that these whites have rejected. In his *Playboy* interview, Marshall McLuhan described this contrary motion thus:

> . . . at precisely the time when the white younger generation is retribalizing and generalizing, the Negro and the Indian are under tremendous social and economic pressure to go in the opposite direction: to detribalize and specialize, to tear out their tribal roots when the rest of society is rediscovering theirs. Long held in a totally subordinate socioeconomic position, they are now impelled to acquire literacy as a prerequisite to employment in the old mechanical service environment of hardware, rather than adapt themselves to the new tribal environment of software, or electric information, as the middle-class white young are doing. . . . This generates great psychic pain, which in turn is translated into bitterness and violence. . . .

Blacks and Indians, he continues, literally cannot afford to repudiate technology and American affluence "because of their inferior economic position." This "lessens the chances for an across-the-board racial detente and reconciliation, because rather than diminishing and eventually closing the sociopsychic differences between the races, it widens them."

The only hope, McLuhan says, in closing the gap lies in the Black Power movement "with its emphasis on Negritude and a return to the tribal pride of African cultural and social roots." Black youth are presently involved in the process of deliberately alienating themselves and other blacks from the values and concepts and culture of Western society. Thus, young blacks and young whites are, to a degree, following parallel courses, going in the same direction. It would seem at this point that black nationalism will be a strong enough force to offset the desires of those blacks who, while not wanting assimilation, want a black American Dream.

Since black and white youth are going in the same general direction, the obvious question is, why don't they get together? Basically, because there is no reason why they should, even if they could. Until whites, including the youth, rid themselves of racism, there is no possibility of even thinking about getting together. At the same time, however, it is necessary that young blacks at least be aware of what is transpiring among white youth. Despite the racism, the white youth culture is valid and if blacks will open themselves to it, they will be afforded insights into America they would otherwise be without. It is these white youth who have been deeper into one aspect of the soul of America than anyone else. They have looked death in the face from their end of the tunnel as blacks have from theirs. At least we can tell each other about the two kinds of deaths. Whites are still incredibly naïve about physical violence and the evil in Western society. Blacks are naïve about what material goods can do to the human soul.

Whether or not blacks will be able to look upon the white youth culture seriously remains to be seen. There are indications that this may eventually happen. Within the white youth culture there are a surprising number of black hippies. Exactly what this means is uncertain. Yet, they are there. The number of young blacks who listen to rock is also not small and, most surprising, the number of black performers who have recorded the songs of white rock composers and performers is significant. Aretha Franklin, the undisputed Lady of Soul, has recorded songs by the Rascals, the Band, Laura Nyro, the Rolling Stones and the Beatles. The Four Tops recorded a Tim Hardin song. Wilson Pickett and Ray Charles have recorded at least one Beatle song each. Nina Simone and Roberta Flack have recorded songs by Leonard Cohen and Bob Dylan. These songs have, of course, become black songs in the transition, but something significant is happening when Aretha Franklin sings "Eleanor Rigby" and sings "I'm Eleanor Rigby." Ultimately, she is, because "I am he as you are he as you are me and we are all together."

It is too much to ask blacks to stop hating young whites so that the new culture might grow strong. It is difficult for anyone. There is nothing to do but for each to continue along his own roads. At least the roads each of us are on, black and white youth, are better than any of the roads traveled by previous generations.

Who Shall
Civilize
the Jungle?

In 1970, with nearly every prominent Black Panther leader in jail, in exile or under close police surveillance, Fred Hampton of Illinois and another Illinois Panther officer were killed by police. The shootings climaxed a year of Panther arrests, raids and killings by policemen all over the country. Hundreds of members of the organization have been indicted and charged with crimes. Some of the arrests were undoubtedly motivated by political considerations. But, politics cuts both ways.

A large number of blacks who are in jail are there for political crimes, only in the sense that a politics of racism made criminality their only out. There are others, some Panthers, who enter a life of crime for political purposes. The seemingly fragile justification that it is an act of politics to take something back from Whitey is sometimes shored up by the intention to organize in jail when arrests come.

Prison authorities have experienced their inability in past years to inhibit the growth of the Muslims within prison walls. Eldridge Cleaver, who was himself politicized in prison, believed that revolutions are hatched either in exile or in jail. To a revolutionary, being in or out of jail differs only in the geography of one's oppression. Policemen, judges, bailiffs, collection agents, prison guards, generals, status-quo-

REGINALD MAJOR

oriented public officials, and citizens content with their lives are all oppressors and counterrevolutionaries.

A University of Chicago law professor, Geoffrey C. Hazard, Jr., also executive director of the American Bar Foundation, attempted to alert the House Committee on Crime during hearings held in July, 1969, that what is happening in the ghettos is: "youth crime is becoming a self-conscious act of political rebellion." These youths, in or out of jail, are the stuff of which black revolution is made, and are the basis of a new politics.

But the call for armed black revolution is hardly new. In 1843, a Presbyterian minister, Henry Highland Garnet, delivered a speech in Buffalo, New York, to a group named the National Negro Committee. His speech, "Call to Rebellion," included the exhortation: "Let your motto be resistance! Resistance! Resistance! No oppressed people have ever secured their liberty without resistance." Garnet, one of the first American black leaders to call for a national liberation struggle, himself carried a gun (which he used to defend himself from a white mob on at least one occasion), called for the establishment of a black press as an effective means of promoting black unity while attacking institutional racism, and attempted to make the black liberation struggle a subject of international interest. He was the American delegate to the World Anti-Slavery Convention and was active in peace movements as well.

Garnet directly influenced John Brown, who not only reprinted the "Call to Rebellion" at his own expense, but directly precipitated the Civil War by attacking Harpers Ferry.

History is repeating itself, and in doing so is underlining the fact that the inability of whites to understand the nature of the frustration of black people is no excuse for the failure to perceive the absolute necessity of developing resistance to all forms of human brutality.

America's present infatuation with law and order is a farce if it is sought by the denial of justice and peace. That infatuation has grown as a reaction to the black's militant thrust toward equality. But the social goals of the Black

Panthers go further than black liberation. They encompass white liberation, national freedom and collective self-respect. Panthers, in describing themselves as the vanguard, insist that it is only by identifying with the need for black liberation that all Americans can free themselves.

The politics of black liberation yield valuable insights about America. Black people are poor, but whites who think of themselves as affluent are to a great extent kidding themselves. By a quirk of statistics, it turns out that fewer than 5 percent of Americans control over 20 percent of the economy, and that the poorest 20 percent of citizens own less than 5 percent of the nation's wealth. Those in between are hardly well off. At least 10 percent of the nation is receiving public assistance, a figure that welfare officials admit could easily be doubled by the simple expedient of extending welfare to everyone who qualifies under the law.

A further comment on America's assumed affluence is revealed by government estimates, which have established an annual income of $10,000 as the figure that would allow a family of four to live modestly. Over 75 percent of American families earn less than $10,000 a year, and whether they know it or not, have not succeeded in achieving a modicum of gracious living.

In sum, the institutions that serve most Americans are less effective in achieving a reasonable standard of living for citizens than the organizations that serve stockholders, giant corporations and the economic empires called conglomerates. What is being termed as a taxpayers' revolt, illustrated by the increasing refusal of Americans to support bond issues and tax increases, seems to be nothing less than people who cannot afford to pay out more money saying so through the use of the ballot.

Whole educational systems are going bankrupt, colleges are not expanding to accommodate the public need for higher education and welfare needs are hardly being met. Hunger is a reality in this rich land, and discontent is wider spread than just among nonwhites.

Black discontent is not an isolated phenomenon. The entire nation is being "niggerized." It is becoming a cesspool, a slum, a crumbling and eroding monument to the rapaciousness with which those with power approach the rest of the nation. Beaches are covered with oil slicks, undisposable garbage clogs overused sewers, the air we breathe is filled with manmade toxins and whole rivers are being converted into receptacles for industrial wastes. Incongruously, one Ohio river was declared a fire hazard, so great was its pollution. The quality of all our lives is being compromised by the greed and insensitivity of a few.

Greed and oppression are major items in the history of this country, as is violence. H. Rap Brown was not at all facetious when he remarked that "violence is as American as apple pie." Long before any college students thought of seizing an administration building, a group of American farmers occupied the courts and refused to let any judicial business be transacted. That was in 1786. The farmers were successful, the taxes that they were protesting were repealed and Shays' Rebellion became history. The middle of the nineteenth century produced a number of riots directed against Irish Catholics; the bloodiest occurred in Philadelphia, City of Brotherly Love, in 1844. About two thousand people were killed in the New York draft riots of 1863, during five days of violence protesting conscription for the Civil War. Rioters were white and northern, and many of their victims were black.

Ten years later, the West Coast experienced a series of riots in which a large number of Chinese were killed. There was also, of course, the genocide that accompanied the conquering of American Indian territory. Beginning in the eighteen nineties, fifty years of labor violence were characterized by shootings, bombings, bloody clashes and virulent police oppression of working people. In the nineteen twenties, there were still more riots, and these resulted in the deaths of several hundred black people.

Violence is apparently on the increase. Over eight thousand people are shot to death annually, and on the average one of every four hundred Americans are either murdered, raped, robbed or beaten. Although Negroes figure in the crime statistics, the truth is that the overwhelming number of violent incidents are the result of white activity.

Much of this violence is the direct result of national policies and police, who ostensibly fight crime, but help to contribute to the figures. The tone for police departments is set in many instances by the FBI, which in numerous ways is both racist and right wing. J. Edgar Hoover, despite evidence to the contrary, has repeatedly asserted that black militance is a major cause of social unrest. He has developed a list of subversive groups that includes the SDS, the Black Panther Party, SNCC, the Revolutionary Action Movement and the Republic of New Africa. Significantly, the police action directed against SDS has been much less extreme than that experienced by the other four groups, which unlike SDS are all black.

The police party line on black militance was demonstrated before a subcommittee headed by Senator John McClellan, in early 1969. Policemen from Oakland and New York, testifying at sessions held two weeks apart, gave almost identical testimony on the Black Panthers.

Imagine, despite the different levels of activity throughout the country, policemen from San Francisco, New York, Chicago, Jersey City, Los Angeles and Oakland had essentially the same thing to say about the danger of the Panthers to internal security. In building their case, incidentally, extensive use of police arrest records was the rule. There was no attempt to note whether the individuals named were convicted or acquitted of the charges. This nationwide oppression of the Panthers indicates that the police establishment has developed a monolithically unified stance against them.

The informed opinions of special investigating commissions have underscored police involvement in perpetuating violence. The National Commission on the Causes and Prevention of Violence issued a report tracing the history of violence in America: "The grievances and satisfactions of violence have so reinforced one another that we have become a rather bloody-minded people in both action and reaction. We are likely to remain so as long as so many of us think violence is an ultimate solution to our problems."

The National Commission on the Causes and Prevention of Violence also noted that the American machinery of justice was fragmented, inadequate and archaic. The commission did not make any specific recommendations about how the nation might go about correcting racial prejudice among policemen, turnstile courts and scandalous jails. They did state:

> Police carry not only the burden of law but also the symbolic burden of all government; it is regrettable, yet not surprising, that particularly the tensions and frustrations of the poor and the black come to focus on the police.
>
> The antagonism is frequently mutual. Racial prejudice in police departments of major cities has been noted by reliable observers. Prejudice compromises police performance. Policemen who systematically ignore many crimes committed in the ghetto, who handle ghetto citizens roughly, who abuse the rights of these citizens, contribute substantially to disaffection with government and disrespect for law.

But police actions are not isolated from other social phenomena. Police departments are part of a national organization with direct links to the army. The Directorate for Civil Disturbance Planning and Operations (DCDPO) was created and incorporated into existing army operations at the Pentagon. A worldwide information complex, geared to give instant data to military leaders, maintains dossiers on one hundred to one hundred and fifty cities. This center retains a small standing army, ready to move into any city where disturbances occur. The army, however, gets most of its information on the potential danger to a city from local police officials.

The police establishment is also linked to big business in a somewhat bizarre fashion. A San Francisco export concern, Polak Winters and Company, filed a suit in United States District Court against Bangor Punta Corporation of Greenwich, Connecticut. Bangor Punta is a conglomerate that had an estimated $260-million income in 1968. The suit estimates that by 1972, public security and law enforcement needs in the United States alone will have a market of $1.5

billion. This revelation becomes shocking when one considers that Bangor Punta has 65 percent of the law enforcement market and specializes in supplying equipment for an entire national police department.

Police armaments that are tested domestically are also exported to other countries (Japan is a leading customer). By exporting police technology, the Americanization of police practices all over the world is a distinct possibility. Of more immediate importance is the implication that the profit motive places up-to-date technological innovations for the control of a civilian population into police hands. With links to the army, big business and traditional conservatism, the police establishment gives every indication of being willing to limit the freedom of all Americans, in a search for law and order.

Even the American Medical Association, an organization that can live with contemporary notions of what law and order should be, has attacked police practices. A survey conducted by the Physicians for Automotive Safety condemned the practice of "hot pursuit" by police seeking to apprehend people suspected of committing misdemeanors. They concluded that: "more than 500 Americans die and over 1,000 sustain major injuries each year as a result of rapid police pursuit of lawbreakers, most of whom are guilty of only minor traffic offenses." Police Departments have ignored these findings and continue to chase whenever they feel it necessary.

Police, moreover, are involved in controlling categories of crime that require more subtle judgments than those available to many patrolmen. They are in charge of anti-obscenity laws, have censoring units zeroing in on books, movies and plays, and enforce antiprostitution laws, usually by arresting the prostitute but not her customer. Most important, police departments generally have a political division, where officers decide what citizens are politically subversive, and what criminal charges can be brought to bear on some of them.

Police are not responsible for all the ills of the nation, particularly those related to race. They are, however, in the position of being able to block effective amelioration of problems by simply enforcing what they consider to be the law or deciding what is moral. Now that they have zeroed in on black militance a crisis has been created.

Who shall civilize the jungle? It shouldn't be police; they don't know how.

The problem is fairly simple. People, a populace, get the kind of police activity they want, up to and including a police state. There are simply not enough guns, or more important, enough people willing to wield them against a population that insists on maintaining control of their police force.

There are enough policemen, however, to effectively limit the actions of those who express dissatisfaction with the quality of their lives, as long as a majority of citizens are satisfied with or uncritical of their life experiences. Unfortunately, the majority (whites) do not equate any unhappiness they might harbor with that articulated by blacks. One of the reasons is that proportionately fewer whites come into any form of contact with police. When they do, the contact is generally devoid of the racist leanings or class hang-ups that many officers display to blacks.

The content, maybe silent toleration, with which most whites approach the police function makes them vulnerable to the notion that blacks tend to attract police attention because of widespread criminality. Even when there is sympathy for the goals of blacks, who in some organized fashion have run afoul of the law, conflict with police is not considered a critical issue. The white citizen might approve of the goals and put down the tactics. Or else, where he feels that police have acted unfairly, he places faith in the court system to ultimately dispense justice to blacks.

Blacks, on the other hand, who experience the loss of friends or relatives through police action, have no real recourse to the courts. The defendant is dead. Twenty-eight Panthers have been killed by police in a two-year period. Blacks have to accept that fact, all the while knowing that many more black men have anonymously gone to their deaths at the hands of police.

Blacks, who are disproportionately victims of the fact that "too often lower criminal courts tend to be operated more like turnstiles than tribunals," consider arrest nothing more than a one-way ticket to jail.

On one level a tremendous amount of black energy is directed toward erasing the race and class distinctions that result in disproportionate contacts with courts, welfare departments, policemen and probation officers. But as long as police effectively serve to contain the boundaries of social protest, they must contend with a gut-level opposition to them as policemen. It is the black community that has pushed most vigorously for effective police reform, and it is this particular item that the society has not seen fit to deal with even on a token basis.

What is necessary is for whites who really feel the need to effectuate law and order to develop an appreciation of how that goal can be reached. Whites can determine the conditions under which black liberation will become a reality. In doing so, whites may discover that they too are being liberated from a slavery that they have been conned into believing is freedom.

The combination of white slavery and police killing upset San Francisco's black community in November, 1969. Someone, black, apparently attempted to fraudulently cash a check for $150 at a downtown branch of Bank of America. He presented the check to a female teller, who grew suspicious and presented the bogus document to one of her superiors. The suspect developed suspicions of his own and decided to leave the bank without the check or the money. He was followed out by a policeman working as a teller.

This policeman was not an undercover agent. He was moonlighting, pure and simple. His life was governed by an inexorable economic situation that made it difficult for him to live in the manner he would like simply by working for the relatively high-paid San Francisco Police Department. He, therefore, picked up a second job.

The bank was delighted with the arrangement. Tellers earn less than highly trained guards, and in this moonlighting officer they had both. Bank robbing has become a favorite indoor sport among a number of people, and a police presence seemed to offer some protection against coerced withdrawals of funds.

It seems clear, though, that the officer in question should not have had to take that job in any capacity other than guard. When he leaped over the counter to pursue the fellow he thought had attempted to bilk the bank, the officer was coincidentally defending his right to work a minimum of sixty hours a week, just to make ends meet. He was possibly fatigued; after all, the work week was fairly long, and he would, therefore, have been operating at less than optimum. But, in accordance with accepted nationwide police practice, he was armed and authorized to discharge that gun under certain conditions, toward anyone suspected of committing a felony. It is a felony, incidentally, for someone suspected of possibly committing a misdemeanor to ignore the commands of an officer. It is in fact a felony for anyone to ignore the commands of an officer.

The officer followed the man he thought to be the suspect into the street and reportedly kept track of him moving through thronged, downtown pedestrian traffic. The chase (conducted at the pace of a fast walk) ended with the suspect receiving a bullet in the back of the head, shot by an officer who said that the suspect had made motions indicating that he might be armed. Result, one dead black man, and one exonerated policeman, who conceivably might be commended in the future for sharp off-duty work, but who has no immediate prospect of making ends meet through working at one job.

While the black experience is a concentrated distillate of the flaws in the society as a whole, police practices reveal the enormity of the problem that must be solved. The armed constabulary, in this context, accurately represents the extent to which government is flawed and is in desperate need of the corrective action of citizens who genuinely desire a government that seeks to improve their lives.

Policing involves much more than crime prevention, the apprehension of felons or the regulation of driving behavior. The Food and Drug Administration, for instance, has police powers, and there is ample evidence to show that it represents more pill-makers than pill-takers. As a result, we have been subjected to a dreary procession of doubtful drugs that have taken their toll of American lives, mental health and in some instances (thalidomide), future generations.

Those policing agencies regulating mass media have not insisted on the public's right to be exposed to a variety of newsworthy informational items. The Panthers are a perfect example. In the main, the impact of their arguments have not reached the general public. What is known about them generally revolves about their position relative to the gun. The speeches of Eldridge Cleaver, the writings of Huey P. Newton, the rationale behind the Panther's ten-point program, the genuine humor with which Bobby Seale has approached the serious business of revolution, the genuine tenderness governing many of the relations among Panthers convinced that an early death is their destiny, the desperate courage required of youth determined to face the overwhelming disapproving force of a society that has betrayed them, their families, friends and aspirations, and the real potential within black circles to ultimately unify behind a Panther-like political orientation, has been presented only in the underground press.

Even those newspapers or television commentators who oppose the excrescence that is the Vietnamese war never speculate on the ultimate racism of a nation that seeks through force of arms to convince a people that it is right that they kill each other. Under these conditions it is hardly to be expected that the media will seriously attempt to get the idea across that killing is an invalid expression of national interest.

The same Internal Revenue Service that comes down heavily on wage earners who illegally try to save a few dollars in tax, openly bargains with the monied persons whom they know have withheld hundreds of thousands of dollars from the public treasury. Despite the obvious fact that the automobile industry is befouling the air, burning up natural resources, creating piles of metallic garbage and producing unsafe vehicles that have, through deaths, injuries and property damage, cost the nation more than the entire industry is worth, it is allowed to make profits rather than being made to pay reparations to those upon whom it has inflicted harm.

Somehow, it is against the law to shoot dice on a street corner, while at the same time the ultimate form of economic legitimacy is the well-heeled crap shooting that goes on in Wall Street-dominated security exchanges. There are agencies that go after the poor suspected of welfare cheating, and others that make sure surplus food is securely locked away. A cosmic form of obscenity is the concept of surplus food, in a nation where there are millions of hungry people.

Democracy—functional, vibrant, participatory democracy—is revolutionary. But it requires well-informed, concerned citizens, who know their rights and who have a capacity to become angry when those rights are violated. The dilemma that blacks confront involves the possibility of violent assertion of their rights to be human or a nonviolent acceptance of the majority's continued silent submission to the ruination of their lives. No one, regardless of ethnic background, is going to escape the political upheaval that is revolution. All that can be done is to determine the style of a revolution that is already in progress.

The Black Panthers can only be controlled by Black People. They can be maligned, killed, misrepresented, ignored, hated, offered bribes by whites, but they can only be controlled by blacks. Issues raised by Panthers do get to blacks, and the attempts to control the party by force of arms only serves to illustrate the necessity of blacks resisting the oppressive social inertia that issues from a people who have, by failing to oppose injustices in their own lives, opted to deny their own humanity.

The young men who were prepared to shoot it out in protection of Cleaver's rights in San Francisco, the eleven Panthers who held off three hundred heavily armed Los Angeles policemen for five hours, the indomitable Bobby Seale, who, manacled, chained and gagged, managed to shout to a court that his rights were being violated, represent a politics of liberation that is impelling in its validity.

The Black Panthers, then, are an organization formed by politically oriented men who, because of their race, class or opinions, were denied the right to present their views as elected representatives of their peers.

And who is more valid? The judge, who in sending Dred Scott back to slavery noted that Negroes had no rights that white men were bound to respect, or Bobby Seale, who in being denied his day in court, attempted to expose the system of justice as a fraud?

Blacks are guided by their experience that the fact of a majority is not a guarantee of rightness. Their political priorities are coming from outside the area with which most whites identify. Blacks have assumed the task of completing the work begun by the revolution in 1776. They have managed to maintain a sense of humor despite humorless enslavement and create a vision of Utopia through a lens formed of the detritus of their slum-bred lives. In their frustration, and by virtue of being the most denied, blacks are attempting to point the nation toward a heightened appreciation of its own humanity.

Such are the Panthers, an organization dedicated to discovering Utopia, by challenging the chaos that is Babylon. They have no questions about who should bring civilization to the jungle which is America. Whites have demonstrated their inadequacy in this area.

Red men were all but eliminated on this continent. Yellow men, needed for the future development of Chop Suey and the then-present need to expand the railroad, were kidnaped and seduced into crossing the Pacific. Mexicans, partial descendants of Europeans and Indians, were also systematically eliminated by a people capable of tolerating fantastic dimensions of evil in the name of racial superiority.

Today, a black time is upon us. "We shall gain our manhood," shouts Cleaver, "or else the world will be leveled in our attempts to do so." That is the prophecy of this age, and the answer to those who question the intent of the Panthers. "By any means necessary," embraces both peaceful means and those that rise from the impelling necessity to counter unreasonable force with politically motivated violence.

The choice is civilization or civil disorder, extremes that Martin Luther King detailed as community or chaos. The black cats and Niggers, born amidst white Americans, trapped between the white heritage of a bloodthirsty history and a tendency toward soul-saving rhetoric, despised, spat upon, considered a creation slightly higher than whale shit, are the natural heirs to the American dream.

The black man, whose need for a sense of his humanity is so compelling that he has produced great men under the most difficult of circumstances, is moving to bring greatness to the American experience. His thrust toward freedom is an ultimate gift to America and the world. If he is denied the opportunity to contribute to the cleaning up of American politics, he will stand in the ghettos of America and evolve into the most determined resister of racist expression that the globe has ever experienced.

The choice between white reactionary styles and a freedom-seeking, non-uptight-about-other-people orientation is what lies before us.

Who shall civilize the jungle? It is obvious. Those who know that the jungle is not a threatening place. Black people, whose ancestors foolishly succumbed to an ego trip, shouted, "Come out of those trees and fight like a man," now know that manhood could have been achieved within those trees and without the political vacuity essential to a culture that has been raised to destroy the strange, the heretical, the different, the darker person, and to characterize those efforts as opposing sin.

No one will civilize if whites fail to recognize and identify with the demands of blacks that they be treated in a civil and human fashion. To destroy black people, a process that has begun with the systematic attempt to repress Panthers, will demonstrate to the world (most of whom are not white), what they must do in order to survive. And, during the ensuing struggle, ghosts of every murdered black will haunt the land, seeking the destruction of those who would assume rule without first seeking the power to rule that is only freely conferred by a free people. It is impossible to suppress freedom and to simultaneously control the urge of men to choose to fight for their humanity. Either the race or racism will be eliminated, and that decision will be made by white Americans.

The Panther, the black cat, is preparing for the worst.

Editor's Note:

In *Soul on Ice,* Eldridge Cleaver speculated on the future of the racial crisis in America in an essay entitled "Convalescence." His point was that (by virtue of the Twist, Elvis Presley and the Beatles), white America had made a "radical break," taken a "revolutionary leap" from its traditional role of "usurping sovereignty by monopolizing the mind" and turned toward the exploration and understanding of the body—a realm heretofore left to blacks, America's "Supermasculine Menials." In Cleaver's view, the phenomenon portended a mediation of the polarized (mind = white, body = black) societal schism fabricated by white males to assure their control as "Omnipotent Administrators"; it foreshadowed a period of convalescence wherein whites shook their asses and discovered the life force of the body and blacks awakened to the powers of the mind. It was "a way station [perhaps the last] on a route traveled with all deliberate speed."

One may or may not agree with Cleaver's analysis of the social upheaval that has moved America's white youth from Comoism to Jaggerism—some would even deny that it represents any significant alteration. Certainly there is some doubt as to whether it is facilitating any new black-white social realignment or is simply the result of other societal changes having scant connection with United States racial conflicts. At any rate, the question of whether a viable communication, rhythmic or otherwise, has been newly established between black and white youth is paramount to the black movement—in any struggle one must recognize his enemies and his allies.

The two essays that follow—one by a white novelist, the other by a black poet—are responses to Cleaver's essay.

Both writers are of the "new generation"; however, their viewpoints are distinctly different. Their responses demonstrate blatant variances on many aspects of Cleaver's contentions and shades of differences on others. Although the essays may not represent, and were not intended to represent, the preponderant opinion of either the black or white majority, they are forthright reactions to the question Cleaver posed, i.e.: Is America headed toward chaos and disaster or the future and life? The content of these reactions provides answers that are manifestations of the authors' perceptions and their cultural backgrounds; the form in which their answers appear reflects the expressive modes (the first—lineal, visually inclined; the second—a rap, orally inclined) that yet distinguishes those respective cultural backgrounds.

The White Niggers
of the Seventies

The definition of life is change. Everything is always growing or shrinking, stretching, pulsing, *moving*. The beat, the rhythm of life never stands still for any of us, and if you screw your eyes shut and turn off your mind to grab a little rest, you soon get run over by the wheel of events and become just another accident of time and space. The young know this, the old have forgotten it. No, rather say they have repressed it, burying it in some atavistic sinkhole of their collective unconscious. With their vested interests, high returns and low risks, they speak of justice, pray for peace and fight for the status quo. All in vain. The beat, as the disk jockeys like to say, goes on and the old are tick-tocked out of the way. New cultures grow and from them come life styles that feed on the dying tissue of traditional ways, manners, morals and values.

To have lived in these dis-United States for the past forty years is to be old. Old in bitter experience, in uncomfortable memories and painful recollec-

SHANE STEVENS

tions. Old in the ways of subterfuge, hypocrisy and compromise. Survival. That's the key word. "What good is life if I'm not in it?" asks the young old-timer. And so he does whatever is necessary in his times in order for him to survive. He goes with the crowd, plays the game, follows the leader. He laughs with his friends, loves his family and kills his enemies. Or his people's enemies, or his society's enemies, or whoever he's told is his enemy: the Japanese, Koreans, Chinese, Cubans, Vietnamese. Odd how the enemies of America always seem to be Asiatic, or at the least, from the nonwhite sector of world population. (Yes, I have heard the stories of America going to war against Nazi Germany and the insane Adolf Hitler. Only the way I heard it, America saved the Big Bomb for the Japanese. And then dropped a second, just to reinforce the moral.)

For the older generations of Americans, there seems to be another enemy right here in their own homeland. Naturally, it's a nonwhite enemy. That helps to keep it in an historical perspective. This enemy, unfortunately, lives here, eats and sleeps here and sometimes, when he can find a job, even works here. This enemy is black, and as every God-fearing white older American knows, black is sin, evil, corruption, damnation. Blackmail, black death, black cat, black-ball, black magic, black sheep. All bad. The American black man. Shades of sin! Don't let him in.

Except he's in already. Yeah. Been here over three hundred years, too. First came here in 1619; that's a whole year before the Pilgrims had their Rock festival. Lessee now, 1619 from 1969, playing it like I was at the Big A watching my dude banging home a winner, that come to, uhh, one-two-three-four-five sawbucks plus three yards on the double O, why, laying all that together make it three hundred fifty years. Howlin' wolf! That's a long mothertime to be in enemy territory. Something's wrong somewhere.

What's wrong is that white America, for all these three hundred fifty years, has treated black America as an enemy, exploiting it whenever possible, killing it whenever necessary. And even when not necessary. Black America fought back; oh yez oh yez, fought back much harder and much more often than the Nat Turner mythmakers (white, naturally) would have us believe. But numerically and strategically it was no contest.

What's wrong is that white America sees the American black man as an enemy in his own land. Sees him as an intruder, a slave at best, scavenger at worst. Sees him as dangerous, wishes he would disappear and dreams of killing him. Yet the American black man will not disappear, and refuses to be killed off. Forget all this nonsense about Africa being the home of America's blacks. Ain't so. America is home. So that makes it a pluralist society. Well, and that's what white America asked for all those centuries and years ago when twenty Africans were traded for food at Jamestown, because those twenty blacks sure didn't ask for it.

What's wrong is that white America has fed itself on its own lies to the point where the present older whites are living so far in the past they'd need Mandrake to lead them back to the twentieth century.

What's right is that this white America is dying. Dying, dying, dead. Dylan said it in "Subterranean Homesick Blues": You don't need a weatherman to know which way the wind blows. Yeah. The wind is blowing good, blowing down the matchbook caretakers of a diseased society, and blowing in a new culture. A youth culture that sees man as good until proved bad, that is color-blind as far as worthiness is concerned, that is spontaneous and mind-free, that is not afraid to love or to question all authoritarianism. A youth culture that is not willing to kill or be killed for spurious motives. A youth culture that is life-centered, not death-oriented. This is what I celebrate. Not the body electric, but the mind alive. The seeking of new avenues to love, to self-awareness and self-fulfillment.

To say that only a minority of America's young people are total activists in the new youth culture is to miss the point. The life style of my generation has already changed immeasurably from that of our parents. The value systems of the older generations—indeed, apparently of all past generations in America—has become irrelevant. The American penchant for material possessions, the various rungs of social worth on the ladder of acceptability, the society-instructed definitions of those things worth knowing and worth doing, the God-given assertion that America's manifest destiny is to save the world for "democracy"—all of these anachronisms are dead and discarded, buried and forgotten. They have proved meaningless in the search for a personal life style that has dignity and some measure of importance to it. In this sense, the youth revolution in America has touched, affected, moved and changed the lives of far more young people than just those with whom it began.

Revolution. The word has a tremor to it, an air of importance. It's much like a gun; when you point it at me, you better use it. And when you say revolution, you better mean it. The only meaning the word has today in the American context is with the youth. There *has* been a revolution in life styles; a significant change—almost a complete overthrow of old values—*has* irrevocably taken place. The drug culture is shifting emphasis inward rather than outward in the search for knowledge, using nonrational ways to discover truth. The love ethic is affirming the intrinsic dignity of human relationships, based on the sanctity of the individual and the efficacy of the personal experience. The new morality is distilling a new wisdom that does not use the deadly rhetoric of the past to build artificial power structures. The rock sound is becoming the politics of joy for the inheritors of the earth. Finally, and perhaps of most importance, the new nation is creating an atmosphere of casual acceptance of interracial situations that is—there simply is no other word for it—revolutionary.

You can write off all the older generations now living in America when it comes to accepting—and treating—the black man as an equal. They just don't buy it. Some of them try but they can't make it, not really. Every black man around knows that. So it's all up to the young. White *and* black. If they can get their shit together, they just might pull it off. They just might make the oldest country in the world seem youthful.

In an essay called "Convalescence," which appears in *Soul on Ice,* Eldridge Cleaver writes of the attempt America has made over the past fifteen years to heal itself: ". . . the history of America in the years following the pivotal Supreme Court edict [Brown v. Board of Education] should be a record of the convalescence of the nation. And upon investigation we should be able to see the Omnipotent Administrators and Ultrafeminines [whites] grappling with their unfamiliar and alienated Bodies, and the Supermasculine Menials and Amazons [blacks] attempting to acquire and assert *a mind of their own.* The record, I think, is clear and unequivocal. The bargain which seems to have been struck is that the whites have had to turn to the blacks for a clue on how to swing with the Body, while the blacks have had to turn to the whites for the secret of the Mind."

Forgetting for a moment the blatant oversimplifications, Brother Cleaver's point is well taken. The landmark 1954 Supreme Court decision *was* epochal, and originated a confluence of mind and body (not to mention a jamming of various organs and nerve endings) that is only now beginning to reach floodtide.

In turning to the blacks for body help, how would the white man be taught? As Cleaver sees it: "It was Chubby Checker's mission, bearing the Twist as *good news,* to teach the whites, whom history had taught to forget, how to shake their asses again. It is a skill they surely must once have possessed but which they abandoned for puritanical dreams of escaping the corruption of the flesh, by leaving the terrors of the Body to the blacks."

Yes, yes, Cleaver's taste for seeing everything in hard black and white is well known, and his view of the dance as being *the* instrument of racial rapprochement is, of course, too baroque for comment. But again, he does have a point. The white man *has* downgraded many functions and movements and pleasures of the body, viewing them as somehow evil. In doing so, he has shortcircuited his emotional switchboard more so, perhaps, than have some other races. And he has had to pay the consequences in fear, in a creeping paranoia that is paralyzing his critical faculties. His sex has become mechanical, his pleasures sedentary, his drives and ambitions uncoordinated. He has, in effect, upset the balance of nature within himself.

There are those who view the history of the past fifteen years in this country as an attempt by the white man to correct that imbalance. Cleaver is one of these; beyond that, he is optimistic about a deepening togetherness he sees between black and white. Toward the end of his essay he suggests how the black man is providing a basis for a new era of racial equality:

". . . In the increasingly mechanized, automated, cybernated environment of the modern world—a cold, bodiless world of wheels, smooth plastic surfaces, tubes, pushbuttons, transistors, computers, jet propulsion, rockets to the moon, atomic energy—man's need for affirmation of his biology has become that much more intense. He feels need for a clear definition of where his body ends and the machine begins, where man ends and the *extensions* of man begin. This great mass hunger, which transcends national or racial boundaries, recoils from the subtle subversions of the mechanical environment which modern technology is creating faster than man, with his present savage relationship to his fellow man, is able to receive and assimilate. This is the central contradiction of the twentieth century; and it is against this backdrop that America's attempt to unite its Mind with its Body, to save its soul, is taking place.

"It is in this connection that the blacks, personifying the Body and thereby in closer communion with their biological roots than other Americans, provide the saving link, the bridge between man's biology and man's machines . . ."

Cleaver is right, of course. Not, I think, in his assessment of the past or present, since I find no basis whatever for his assumption that the white man has been knowingly seeking to bridge the racial gap, but in his projection for the future. That is to say, until now the two races have been coming closer together in a manner not exactly calculated to engender optimism. The black man has let it be known that he is a man, and the white man has let it be known that he is in charge. They have squared off, each against the other, unleashing mighty blows of oratory. If words were bullets, America would be a bloodbath now. And if the words were of love, hate would still be running rampant right now, which it is. Except among the young. And there's where my glimmer of hope appears, small though it may be.

Cleaver is a politician. I'm not. He obviously sees, as all politicians must, that optimism is the cornerstone of success in public life. I'm a novelist; I distrust the fashionable. I'm writing these words in the last month of the last year of the sixties, and what I see is a country divided into two camps, separate and unequal. The President's Commission on Civil Disorders had it right. "White society is deeply implicated in the [black] ghetto. White institutions created it, white institutions maintain it, and white society condones it." The commission concluded that the solutions are thirty years behind the problems.

Maybe they are. But if there is any solution at all, it will have to be the straightforward one of people to people. This is what the new life style of the young is all about, and so I have hope. It's a hope grounded in fact—the fact of this generation's very existence—and it has nothing to do with today's America cleansing itself of its prejudices, guilt and assorted hang-ups. That game is over, and the America of today will soon be over, too. It has to do with tomorrow's America. The America where the students now smoking grass will be the judges and lawmakers, where the ghetto kids now hanging around the streetcorners will have good jobs based on their abilities, where the blacks and whites now making it together will bring up interracial families free of the bullshit that emasculated a dozen generations before them.

When I was a kid roaring down the Harlem nights—and even later when I was loning it through all the ghettos and Capetowns of America—the feeling was that the only way the two races could live in peace was if white and black, by the thousands and millions, would get together: kiss, fuck, marry, make babies, get families going so that skin coloring would become meaningless. The word is miscegenation, though I didn't know the word then. Everybody I ever talked to believed this, everybody knew this was the only way to beat a nearly four-hundred-year-old curse.

Nothing has changed. Except that now thousands of young people are living a coffee-and-cream life, and liking it. And that's the beginning of the biggest change this country has ever seen. It's also the beginning of the end for white racist America.

Scene: An apartment in Washington's inner city. Janet is married to Bill, they have two kids. Janet's white, Bill is black as a spade jack. They're thinking about moving to a Virginia suburb. A money suburb. Their chief worry is finding a good apartment building where there are other young people. Even then, they'll have to put up with static from the older townspeople. "Screw 'em," says Bill, "they got to die before me and then I can piss on all them over-thirty farts." Bill is twenty-four, Janet twenty-three. Together they're ready to take on anything. Or anybody over thirty.

Scene: A street corner on Chicago's exclusive Lake Shore Drive. Two black dudes catch the eye of two well-dressed white sexteens. The dudes start their rap; the girls giggle, enjoying themselves. The man in blue sees this, walks over, asks if the dudes are bothering them. The girls look at him as if he's dirt, ostentatiously take the dudes' hands and they all walk away, laughing at the Man.

Scene: A small restaurant in Salt Lake City. Coffee-and-cream couple sit in a booth, eating burgers. She was brought up a Mormon, her parents are good God-fearing religious people. He's a college student, moving around the country during the summer. They met at a Salt Lake college party, now they're making it together. She'll go away with him when he moves on to California and back to school. Someone points out to her that the Mormons regard blacks as inferior, being considered descendants of Cain. What does she think about that?

Her answer is clear and simple. "Religion sucks."

Scene: A bar on New York's Lower East Side. It's owned by a black man. Black studs are in and out all night, eyeing the foxes, most of whom are white. Eventually everybody finds somebody. Happens every night of the week.

Scene: A coffee shop around the corner from the bar. Three young white dudes and their black foxes are jamming at a table. They all live together in a big loft on East Broadway. The girls have lived with other whites before, the boys with other blacks. They all feel comfortable. Why? "You don't have to handle all that heavy shit," says one. What shit? "All that middle-class guilt jazz that comes from being only with your own image."

Scene: A park in Kansas City. Two young white girls wheel babies in cribs. Older people pass by, look in at the babies, prepared to smile, then see they are black, hold back the smile. They walk on, wondering what the white girls are doing with those little colored brats. It never occurs to them that the girls could be the babies' mothers—which they are.

Scene: A pizza parlor in Berkeley. Beautiful blonde sits alone at outdoor table, eating pizza. White dude walks over, starts rapping. She says nothing. Soon a black dude comes by, over to the table, and the fox jumps up and gives him a soul job. The white dude grins, picks up his ego and moves on. Meanwhile, over in one corner he's already spotted this creamy black fox . . .

Scene: The Woodstock rock feast in Bethel, New York. Maybe a half-million kids around. A lot of fuck-suck going down over the weekend. Over by a little pond there's a coffee-and-cream scene. Suddenly a white couple walk by, hand in hand. At least three kids call out, "Racists."

Scene: A black Santa Claus sits in his chair in a fashionable department store in St. Louis. In front of him stretches a long line of girls and boys waiting to sit on his lap. Most of them are white. The boys look to be about five to ten. Some of the girls are at least fourteen. A few of them already have good-sized jugs. One wonders what they hope to feel sitting on a black Santa's lap.

Final Scene: A bit of graffito on a wall of a Detroit diner reads "Jimi Hendrix and Mick Jagger are easy lays." What's so special about that? Nothing much, except it was written in the *men's* sandbox, not the women's. I mean, things are really *coming together*.

If sex is the drive that's taking youthful black and white to their much celebrated destination of togetherness, politics is the vehicle. Not politics in the narrow sense of votes and public office, but in the overview of what kind of existence will be shared. Here again, the enemy is the older segment of the population, the established order of things, the status quo, the parents, the System, the Establishment. It's not working, cry the young, and so it must go. It's oppressive and exploitative and reactionary. All this may sound familiar because black militants have been sounding it for years. But now it is the war cry of the whole mass of angry youth, more white than black, and they intend to do something about it. In 1968, at New York's Columbia University, there was what can only be called a youth rebellion. (I use the word *rebellion* not in any dramatic sense but only as a properly descriptive term.) At the Chicago Democratic Convention, what went down in the streets and parks and hotel lobbies was a youth rebellion. The 1969 People's Park uprising in Berkeley was, again, a youth rebellion. There may well have been rioting at all three events (I was at the Columbia and Chicago blowups and can attest to the fact of massive police rioting at both), but rebellion is what it was all about. The vast black ghetto rebellions of 1964–1967, in which black people of all ages participated, have given way to campus and public affair uprisings, in which only young blacks and whites participate; separately, perhaps, but equally. The shift has been dramatic.

I'll put it another way. For the past decade and more, the struggle in America has been between black and white. One result has been a lot of laws that sound very good and do less good. A much more important result has been the emergence, finally and permanently, you better believe it, of black self-pride. That struggle between black and white is now largely over. It had its day, made its moves and took whatever it could. The new fight—the real honest-to-God revolutionary struggle—is between the young and the old.

Surprising? Not at all. Think along Marxist lines for a moment. In the underdeveloped countries of the world, the struggle is still between the ruling exploitative class and the working exploited mass. But in superdeveloped countries such as America, the working class itself is part of the establishment, part of the ruling clique. Damn right! When a country's economic base has been broadened to the point where the little people have some possessions, they're going to guard those possessions with their very lives. So the working man keeps blacks and other minorities out of his union, buys a gun to protect his house and car (although he claims it's to protect his wife and virgin daughters) and votes reactionary. The whole labor movement is part of the system, and proud of it. Everybody with a vested interest— working class, managerial middle class and the power people —is part of the system and will fight to keep the status quo. The only ones not in the system are the young and the really poor (those with no possessions and no means of getting any), a great many of whom are nonwhite. The poor could be a force for change in a rebellion, but many of them are old and their juices have run dry. That leaves the young, not as a poor oppressed class but as a youth oppressed class, with different ideas, values and goals but no power to implement them. In strict Marxist terms, then, the conflict between young and old is total. The inevitable winner? That shouldn't be hard to figure out.

Bringing it all home now: the young people in America, and apparently in many countries, have developed a life style that is vastly different from and in many instances, directly opposed to that of their parents. Part of their style celebrates total freedom of activity with blacks. This puts the black struggle for equality where it belongs: as part of the youth movement. It's the young, after all, who will be making all the changes. A minority of these young people are radical activists, intent on taking the fight to the enemy, to those in power, i.e., the old. The majority as always is nonviolent, at least collectively. But that minority is becoming larger as society resorts to more repressive measures in defense of itself.

The central question for our times, the crucial overriding question that will affect all our lives and determine whether some of us will live or die, is this: Should the youth rebellion be revolution or evolutionary? It's as simple, and as complex, as that. Should it be direct confrontation or culture manipulation? Should it use violence or eschew violence? Should it attack incessantly or wait patiently for its day to come? For society, the implications of the answer are horrendous.

The young man lit another smoke. The basement was cold and he had on only a sweater. The other people in the room watched him, listening to what he had to say, nodding in agreement as he spoke of the enemy's latest moves. The Chicago conspiracy trial was a farce, as expected. The drug busts were continuing. Underground papers were being suppressed. College administrations were admitting only the athlete type; nine-tenths of the freshman class at Columbia were out-and-out jocks. Countermoves were clearly called for; perhaps a bit of surreptitious activity, something to keep up the momentum of the struggle. The young man looked around him at the faces of the other young men and women in the cold basement room. "Now," he said quietly, "suppose a few of us got some dynamite and started putting bombs in government buildings . . ."

What do you say when someone preaches mass violence? Do you point out that the enemy—America, the older people in power—is the architect of violence? Should you? Do you point out that to use violence is merely to copy the enemy, and therefore to be no better? Should you? And if you do, will anyone listen anymore?

I have been shot, stabbed, beaten, gassed, stomped, whipped, jailed and had acid thrown on me. I have smelled death, seen its shadow and heard its cry. Violence has been my natural playground, and I know little about it. And about the darker side of violence, too, the violence that is within oneself. It's just beneath the surface, lurking there, waiting, always ready to smash, to destroy. Within each of us is this terrible beast; its screamings are maddening and, sometimes, unbearable. Then the violence erupts. The results are always tragic.

When the violence of a whole people erupts, look out, man.

There is another urge within each of us: the urge to create. It is, of course, the opposite of the destructive force, and the battle within is constant. Since it is so much easier to destroy than it is to create, perhaps that is why man is so good at killing. It's a pity. The life style of the young, for example, has already begun to change the face of America through the creative process. Who is to say whether violence helped or hindered? But one thing is certain sure: direct confrontation is deadly to all concerned. Violence leads to more violence, and with each escalation the terror mounts. And then it is too late.

Perhaps for many people in America (young and old) it is already too late.

I'm in the Bridgeport, Connecticut, train station. In the waiting room. A small cop with a big gun is strutting around, a peacock in blue, with a bright blue nametag pinned on his plumage. Several dozen people wait, perhaps for a train already overdue, perhaps for other people. A dude and his fox sit across from me. He's black, maybe twenty-one, she's white, maybe nineteen, and they're holding hands. They seem to be waiting for someone. Everybody stares at them. This is suburban Connecticut, not whore-city New York; what the hell is this? But the kids are dressed well, obviously not hippie types. The cop can't find anything to lay on them.

A man walks into the waiting room. He's well built, well dressed, his manner is money. His eyes flick over the crowd, pick out the kids. Clamping a smile on his tanned face, he walks over to them. The fox jumps up, gives him a kiss, calls him father. Then she introduces her dude. She calls him Thomas. Father shakes hands with Thomas. Everybody's nervous. Then the fox says she's going to fix her makeup. She gets her bag, gives her dude a smile and trots off. As far as she's concerned, Father and Thomas have now been introduced and they can just talk together as two men do. She's so young, and I feel sorry for her.

Father stands there. Thomas stands there. They both look after her, then there's nothing to look at. They're going to have to look at each other. Father is probably a big advertising executive or maybe a bigshot lawyer; his hair looks wise, his eyes old. He's tough. Thomas is black. He's tough, too.

They face each other. Thomas is cool, he's the new breed. He knows the only thing to expect from older whites is trouble. He says nothing. Father is trying to be cool, too. If it wasn't for his daughter, he'd kill this black sonofabitch. Better, he wouldn't even notice him. But he's got to make a move. He loves his daughter, wants to save her. Maybe if he plays along he can work something out. What he *won't* do is scream and holler and forbid her to see this nigger. He knows what *that* would do. He's no dope, he reads *Time* every week.

Father broadens his smile, puts sincerity in his eyes; his silk suit ripples with laughter and good feeling. By God, he'll show that daughter of his how a real man plays the game. He'll snow this black bastard with smooth footwork, and then knife him when he can.

With all the man-to-man intimacy he can put into his voice, Father looks at Thomas and says, heartily, "When Carol wrote us she was bringing you from college for the holidays, the first thing we did was send our colored maid home for a week. We didn't want you to feel uncomfortable."

I saw the dude's eyes harden into knives and I knew we were all one step closer to violence.

Convalescence – Compared to What

In the beginning was the rape
And the rape was labored
And the embryo was cleaved
From the womb
And the painful journey
Across the ice
Began

perhaps the biggest question in the modern world
is the definition of a genius—huemanity. and the
white man is no hueman. it's sheer stupidity for
america to be in vietnam—win, lose (which we are
all doing) or draw—because only david can win when
goliath accepts the challenge. it's like men playing
women in basketball—after all they are men. but
it's questionable if the honkie has a mind, he is an il-
logical animal. animals in their natural environment
have friends and enemies; live in a circumscribed
place; travel by one or two methods—like if they swim

nikki Giovanni

117

and fly they don't run; create little animal communities; live and die. the honkie has defied all this. and forced us to defy it. the honkie can eat anything with immunity—witness pigs, snakes, snails, each other, their children—and survive. they have made one form of cannibalism a love act; which just has to be a comment on their ability to understand word meanings. it's difficult to define a honkie. like we all remember zombie movies. the big black dead things under the bidding of the evil scientist moving around in the jungles of Haiti or some island (it was always an island) hating themselves for what they are but powerless to put their bodies down to rest. generally an ugly honkie woman, which of course is redundant, comes along who is taken to the zombie hideout and wild bill hickock in safari hat and bushjacket follows her, finds the secret to killing the zombie (how can you kill something already dead?) and runs back to civilization. now the zombie is a drink. you order it when you really want to tie one on. wouldn't it be marvelous when we can run to the neighborhood bar and say "give me a double honkie on the rocks, sam," and have the bartender pour something into a glass and shake it up? something needs to shake up the honkie. and a lot of negroes too.

when someone looks at the Watusi and thinks that's the totality of our contribution to the world we realize we are in trouble. not that we are against the Watusi—personally we favor ass shaking under even the most mundane circumstances —but the Watusi is a religious dance performed ritualistically by the high priest and priestess of soul. and just as the roe-man catholic church will not allow the unanointed to partake of the blood and body we should set up the same standards. a people cannot accept as a sign of health nonbelievers practicing their service. this is the crisis harold cruse speaks of and a gross abdication of our duties. those of us who have studied and feel compelled to speak on issues should speak the whole, not the hole, truth.

o ye of little faith and less knowledge; let us venture forth into the night; you with your fanon and i with my twat in the hand.

in the beginning was the man and the man was Black and the Black man was a good man. in the beginning was the woman and the woman was Black and the Black woman was a good woman. they had children; planted; reaped; lived; died. maybe drank a little bali hai, were late on the rent; probably had some kind of car; educated the children— were men and women. Black and proud, "say it loud." they meditated on the sun and planets—created a numbers system; meditated on the earth and figured if they could get a lever they could tilt it. figured out how deep was the ocean; how to mummify people; that anacin was the best thing for a headache (*"butter? butter? bitch you know we ain't had no butter since yo daddy left us!"*); charted the seasons; figured out astrology—the sphinx is virgo and leo no matter what honkies say about them not going together; lived in peace; blended with the earth; had children . . . lived . . . died . . . continued. then, buffy tells us, a buzzard came along, sucked the eggs and changed the story.

man can't separate the mind from the body, sex from salvation, food from thought—the supermasculine menial does not exist. there is no such thing as the omnipotent administrator —what is a superbrain? the pope is the queen of the earth. we are a complete people ready and able to deal completely with tomorrow.

we are lovers and children of lovers. we are warriors and children of warriors. but we don't send children to war. no crusades to hold back the muslim tides. no crusades to hold back the union forces. the child's place is in the home. though we, as children, seized the initiative here in america. the Black family in america has never been declining. when the honkie speaks of the deteriorating negro family he's wrong on all counts. we are not negro. we are not deteriorating; our structure has always been the extended family—many generations living under one roof. our structure has generally been matrilineal though seldom matriarchal. what does the Black woman have to be powerful with/over? if ever you see a powerful nonwhite know that you are seeing a powerful negro. then ask yourself . . . what's a negro?

the honkie is the best mythologist in creation. he's had practice cause his whole wrap is to protect himself from his environment. after generations of lying he does it by second nature. and his first nature is so unnatural that we aren't surprised. "fish gotta swim, birds gotta fly"—honkies gotta lie. i'm telling you why.

Black people are calypso singers, call us signifiers, carolyn rodgers, and larry neal says shine swam on. rap brown played ball in central park and shine swims on. the ultrafeminine and the supermasculine menial—no good. i can't use it. "try to make it real compared to what?" it ain't real—we can't even pronounce the words they and some of us are using to describe us. *"what you mean castrated?" "oh yeah. well i been that."* bullshit. try to make it real. *"my mother did what? man, you better watch yo mouth." goddammit!* compared to what? (un)les McCann can't. honk on pharaoh —that's for real. compared to anything. sock it toward me now.

oh we're so angry with you america, ask buck white. "i gotta live the life i sing about in my songs." marion williams and the sweet inspirations. electric mud and the dells saying "oh what a night." they were in washington dc april 5, 1968. Souls on ice, but "to be black" don lee says "is to be very hot." the age of the cool went out when honkies learned to say "dig" with their eyelids lowered. all we got left is motherfucker. f.(or) u(se) (of) c(arnal) k(nowledge). they can never get that together.

a slave is defined by his duties. and none of us are free. the guns should be toward the west. point them toward navarone. Nix (on) him. spear o agnew.

won't we ever learn? elijah says we are what we eat. it's overdue time to close the doors. it's overdue time to say "which nigger is our nigger." that's all that matters. Support our own. look out for our own. yeah, turn the system Black. don't be afraid of Black folks. don't be afraid of yo mamma. she ain't the one who put you in this trick. but she's the one who'll get you out. and we aren't speaking generically. we are all fathers and mothers. mother is the earth. father the tools to fertilize her. we/they go hand in hand.

in the beginning of the honkie the word was god and the word was white. the paper was white so the word couldn't be seen but only felt. take away the damned and you get evil. DEVIL. take away the damned. some were taught the devil is Black. we're taught he's red. by any definition of devil *she's* got to be white. only the devil could cause so much heartache.

> roaches are red
> the sky is now blue
> if you ain't gone by night
> we're gonna lynch you.

the original white poem. and some Black folks think they can write.

it's a cinch we didn't need to read their shit. why would dostoevsky need to write crime and punishment? for the same reason shakespeare needed to write—not to pass information but to pass time. there are no great honkies—anything that excludes our existence is not great. anything that sheds a negative light on us isn't great. faulkner was a racist. not even a great racist—just a southerner who had no useful skills. didn't even write well. the best you can say for an imitator is that he copies well. for true knowledge we must go to the source. camus and sartre dig on existentialism cause it relieves them of guilt and allows them to colonize fanon and other Blacks under the name of philosophy. without existentialism they would just be honkie colonizers. existentialism became popular after world war two when it was obvious that the world had changed colors. german collaborators, honkies who refused to speak out for the jews (though speaking out wasn't nearly ever going to be enough) jews who refused to speak out for the jews all turned to a philosophy that would allow them to be responsible for the world in general and nothing in particular.

Black groups digging on white philosophies ought to consider the source. know who's playing the music before you dance. someone's poem said before you go to the water know who invented the beach. brothers digging on class struggle ought to go to check out African communalism. that warmed over communism which allowed russia to become a modern-industrialized-capitalistic state isn't for or about us. it's just an old way of colonizing us. *"pussycat pussycat i love you"* and some of us are falling for that. some of us seem ready to accept the essence without performing the act. can't be done. if they had such great minds how come their country is falling apart? james earl jones notwithstanding—america is the great white hope. and she's building a country home in south africa where the weather is cooler. and people talk about not accepting dirty money. all money is dirty. dirty, lazy, filthy lucre. money don't work. money don't sing. money don't dance. can't keep you warm. money is a leech. and we drain ourselves to obtain her. have fallen in love with her. will put none other god before her. try to make it real. compare the gold in fort knox in bars with the way our bodies used to shine with ornaments. yeah we are the body and the blood. we are the salvation. but we too need a transplant. vital organs cannot survive in a decaying body.

melvin tolson says a civilization is in decline when we (they) begin to judge it. the visigoths didn't destroy rome, they just got there in time to claim historical credit. who will get credit for america? that's what the struggle is all about. some say niggers twisting will cause the decline—some say that will save it. but this old body is dying all on its own and we must decide if we are going to take credit for giving it its last kick or for being the last group to try to save it. if i saw a sick old white lady on her way to a convalescence home i'd kick her in the ass and rob her of the twenty cents her dollar is worth—and be proud that i did it. no sense trying to save sick old white ladies. try to make it real. young white people will even kick an old sick white lady on her way to the convalescence home because they want to take credit for being the cause of the fall. compared to what? there was peace after the fall of rome.

roads fell into disuse. weeds covered them. the aqueducts dried up. the soldiers turned their swords to plows. there was no central authority. there was no standard. southern italians were glad rome was dead. they went back to drinking wine, having babies, educating children. living. dying. they spoke italian. roman mercenaries in france stopped collecting taxes. learned french. starting drinking wine. people crossed the channel. people moved into the black forest. the visigoths moved on. and all was quiet on the western front. then some bright dude decided to write a book in vernacular. in italian and a renaissance was born. what had been a period of peace was deemed the dark ages. what had been a democratic period was called anarchy. the rich got poor and the poor got happy. and happy got his ass kicked for coming to the neighborhood. you see it now. the Black renaissance is born. joy to the world.

leroi jones moved uptown. wrote plays in the vernacular and a people found our voice. the idea and the essence had finally formed the man. but the separation was never mind from the body. it was the body from the function. the mind always knew what needed to be done. it wasn't a stupid nigger that fucked with nat turner. it wasn't a stupid nigger that killed malcolm. it's too easy to say how dumb we are. all we got is rhythm. giving the twist to the world will not change that world. and it's far from what we have given. our bodies—in fields, in offices, in laboratories, in beds, in harlem, watts, accra, londonparisromecincinnati—laid to sacrifice will not change the world.

young whites deciding to get hold of our rhythm and fuck will not change the world. it's a physical change and chemical warfare is needed. we need to put a hurting on the world. and all our intellecting bout changes gonna come "yeah baby let me . . . let me baby" will not change the world. swapping sweat or spit let alone wallowing in the shit together may at best allow some honkies to sing the blues—which we should all do all the time if we knew what we don't want to know. the blues, mae jackson tells me ain't what they used to be—done gone and got americanized. and we know that's a shame. come telling mae to stay in school. ain't that a bitch. her what never went to no institution at all, telling her to stay in school and the most tragic thing that happens in america is that there is an accident on the pneu jersey turnpike.

ever think about waking up facing lieutenant william l. calley? well we better be thinking bout it cause they gonna bring that cracker home as punishment for being so stupid. gonna force that cracker to listen to the temps saying i can't get next to you. and calley'll be nodding "you said it nigger."

it's all there in the big black book called whatever happened to cracker america? ruth ain't no baby and her daddy would rather you not eat it—some things are just bad form. squash it together and you get bath. squash it at all and you'll need one.

the biggest lie in creation is you shouldn't try to keep up with the joneses. leroi, sandy, they mama and daddy are something to aspire. the cracker will take everything away from you if you don't be careful. woodie king is pure mahogany. the single most important theatrical event aside from watts, newark and detroit was his production of *slave ship*.

it's so easy to deal off the top. sly says dance to the music. a compelling call to do the freedom walk. but we still dealing on the catch-up. crackers have taken our blues and gone. langston saw it long time ago. taken our blues and put long hair on it. electrified it. they gonna go in for electric dicks next. gonna put them at thirty-three rpms. all they gotta remember to do is turn the heart up to excitement turn the brain to profanity. ain't gonna be much running off natural rhythm. just like anton dvořák took our spirituals and put them in symphony they putting our blues in symphony hall. yes they is—saw the sign up in newark. you see it now (the grateful dead) living proof. of the grateful dead. give a cracker a break—in the neck. and pan broil it with black eyes of sympathetic niggers, should make a good meal for the conjure man. try to make it real.

niggers got a natural twist, especially when we hanging from a wild oak tree. ever hear a real Black person extol the virtues of nature? if you do you'll know it's a negro talking. nature ain't natural here. growing big Black niggers from trees. running down country roads. trying to make it to the swamp. niggers love cement. and there's a reason. if little old men with eight heads came from mars new yorkers would send lindsay down to see what they want. absolute faith in the new politics. rah-rah lindsay. anyone nixon hates has got to be good. apollo got nothing to do with space, ask any Black kid from 110th street to 155th. the apollo now features dionne warwick with her love show.

determined weakness will triumph over the most brilliant, strong willed purist. there's something about weakness that always seems to make it prevail. call it arrogance. most strong people think they can reason with the weak—call it noblesse oblige. most strong people think the least they can do is bend a little—call it illogic. most strong people have no real knowledge of how their strength is used against them. the cracker is a weak being. so is the negro. both sap the energies of Black people. the best anyone can do when dealing with weakness is to get as far away from it as possible. learn to steel yourself against terms like evil (the weak always tell the strong it's evil to be strong). learn to say "that's true" when the weak say "you don't love me." but mostly learn to deal with other strong people.

jesus on the cross knows the weak have a league, a thursday night weak club, where they devise new and exciting ways to trap the strong. and we accept it. the weak have made selfish the worst possible name to be called. couple selfish with nigger and there is no lower animal under allah's wig. the weak have made cleanliness next to godliness and god a green faggot who fucked nature and set the world in motion. the weak have made weakness a religion. the weaker you are the more you have a right to drain the strong. the weak worship weakness. they thrive on it. they love it. next to death weakness is all they respect. you are what you love. the weak have weakness built into the system. there's no way to beat the system. there's no way to change the system. only you change. only you begin to think it's not so bad. only you become weaker because the weak have made strength mean ineffectualness, have made it mean exile, have made it mean jail, have made it mean loneliness, misunderstanding, negativeness. the only good strong person is a dead strong person and weakness kills us dead. god is dead. jesus is dead. allah is dead. king is dead. malcolm is dead. coltrane is dead. dolphy is dead. evers is dead. and we write poems to them. sing songs to them. pour gin libations to them. miss them. quote them. while we don't give a kind word to mingus, the aylers, aretha, ameer baraka, adam powell.

like we don't know what mess james brown is going through. like we don't know how a.d. king died. like we don't like each other cause we look alike. and like the book says "nothing black but a cadillac" niggers ought to be buried in cadillacs, cause that's what's killing us. gm, brooks brothers, lord & taylor, vw's, carrier air-conditioning, philco new color tv with the works in a box—does your box work when you want it to? get a philco for your box. we've got to quit worshiping weakness. we've got to quit understanding it. we've got to quit accepting it. we've got to be strong. in a world where the weak function—the strong must not function. we need togetherness to decide what we will do when they are gone. and we must help them go.

we need to devise a way to put Black teen-age girls to work on the trains. old Black people traveling on the east coast take their lives in their hands. are unable to make changes of trains; in the south and west buses are full of our elderly people. why can't young ladies ride the trains/buses for the express purpose of helping these people. why don't bus companies provide space for them and the state pay them to travel with our elderly citizens? it would help make the elders more comfortable. why don't we have our young men with some kind of machine cleaning the subways? that could be a twenty-four-hour thing. the subs are filthy and unsafe. why not put our youngsters to work for a four-hour shift and the state pay them to do it? new yorkers will suffocate before the bomb drops. why don't we close the streets, plant grass and leave the avenues for traffic? we need to outlaw cars in the cities. transportation could then be by bus with alternate avenues running up and down. you would never be more than a block from where you're going. traffic jams would be no more. the air would be cleaner. our children would have someplace to play. we need in all the big cities to have daily garbage and trash collection. we need to make the buildings we live in safe and habitable. we need to put our women to work sewing curtains, making quilts, cooking, keeping house. our men need to repair, renovate, renew the neighborhood. we need to abolish by declaration private everything—housing property, companies, clubs, you name it—it should go. everything should be in trust for the people. and what the people don't keep up we don't need. we need to spend as much money feeding people as we do starving them. we need to spend as much time devising ways for people to live as we do for killing people.

crackers invented napalm which is so hot it can melt your skin but they can't deal with a decent ice defroster when it snows. we need a shift in priorities. and only we can bring it. if it can be brought. and not by taking on their weakness but by building our own nation. and if a nation can't be built here, by preparing to live without the unessentials which we've never had and are better off without. we may in fact miss the refrigerator, but compare that to air pollution. it all goes together. the refrigerator you need today is keeping nixon in office. will put agnew in office. this is the fall of america. the kennedys were the gracchi brothers; america is rome. the end is the beginning. we must think small, organize small, do little things to chip away at this monolith and elvis presley ain't gonna make it easier. we must recognize that most countries could fit into any american state. america is an unnatural city/state run by unnatural people. we must huddle together in our similarities, develop our language, develop our life style, quit trying to impress the cracker and try to be happy. we must bring on the dark ages, where dark people rule. where, better still, there is no rule—only Black people living giving birth rearing children dying continuing in a natural way the life pattern. we need new definitions and the twist ain't got nothing to do with it. it's time to work to pull down the walls—yeah, it's time for atlas to shrug, so that atlas junior can live.

Seigismundo's Tricycle

DRAMATIS PERSONAE

EDGAR WHITE

Seigismundo
Old white man on a silver tricycle. He wears a long
frock coat which he rolls up in the back in order to
pedal tricycle effectively. On the handle bars hangs a
lit lantern and a little bell which he (Seigismundo)
rings at his entrance and exit. When he halts tricycle
he puts on his buskin-shoes, and leaves them behind
at end.

Privie
A Negro who walks with the aid of crutches. His
feet are padded with bandages. He wears a long robe
of many colors. He too is old but seemingly not as
fatigued as Seigismundo.

ACT I

Scene I

The setting is a gray mist-filled marsh (possibly in New Jersey). The two figures of the old white man on a silver tricycle and his companion and servant on crutches are seen moving across marshes. On stage the white man comes out first. Pedals his bike wearily, making virtually no progress. He regards his location and calls to PRIVIE, *who comes slowly on crutches. On his back* PRIVIE *carries a small knapsack.*

SEIGISMUNDO
Privie. Privie, come along now. Good God: so very lazy. You would think he'd be eager to find out where we are. Privie!

PRIVIE
Coming, Seigismundo.

SEIGISMUNDO
Seigismundo? You're calling me by my first name now.

PRIVIE
I didn't think it would matter now.

SEIGISMUNDO
Some things matter, no matter what.

PRIVIE
No matter.

SEIGISMUNDO
What?

PRIVIE
What?

SEIGISMUNDO
I'm so tired. Give me the bit of chair.

(PRIVIE *takes sack off and takes from it a small folding stool such as children sit on. He sets it up.*)

SEIGISMUNDO

We've come very far.

PRIVIE
(*Sits on ground and puts on buskins.*)
Not very far, really.

SEIGISMUNDO

It seemed terribly far to me. This time I know we didn't go in a circle because I made sure to always keep that mountain on my right side.

PRIVIE

What mountain?

SEIGISMUNDO

That one over . . . (*He looks about him, startled.*) Wasn't there a mountain to our right?

PRIVIE

I didn't see any mountain; just flat land.

SEIGISMUNDO

Well, what the devil happened to the mountain?

PRIVIE

There was no mountain, Seigismundo.

SEIGISMUNDO

Don't tell me. I kept looking at it over my shoulder. I kept saying to myself: Keep your bearing, Seigismundo. You'll get to some kind of fortress soon.

PRIVIE

Well, I sure didn't hide it any place.

SEIGISMUNDO

Of course you didn't hide it. You couldn't hide a mountain. I know that I'm not crazy after all. (*Pause.*) I don't think.

PRIVIE

Well, we'll just have to keep going in the direction that we're heading.

SEIGISMUNDO

Yes, but which way is that, dammit?

PRIVIE

I don't know. There must be something someplace.

SEIGISMUNDO

Why?

PRIVIE

What do you mean, why?

SEIGISMUNDO

Why does there have to be something someplace?

PRIVIE

I don't know. You're the one that's supposed to be leading.

SEIGISMUNDO

Oh, I'm depressed again.

PRIVIE

Why are you depressed now; it's still light out. You don't usually get depressed until it's dark.

SEIGISMUNDO

What the hell do I care whether it's light or dark. I'm depressed.

PRIVIE

All right. No need to shout.

SEIGISMUNDO
(*Exasperated.*)
And you, you're more of a botheration to me than an aid.

PRIVIE
Then why don't you leave me?

SEIGISMUNDO
I will some day.

PRIVIE
Well, why don't you? Just get up on your little tricycle and haul away.

SEIGISMUNDO
Never mind telling me to get on my tricycle. Just . . . just . . . remember your place, that's all. (*Pause.*) Have we anything left?

PRIVIE
Anything left?

SEIGISMUNDO
To eat, I mean.

PRIVIE
(*Opening sack.*)
Hmmm. A few nuts.

SEIGISMUNDO
I thought the world would have been grateful for my birth.

PRIVIE
And six figs.

SEIGISMUNDO
I did what they wanted. I got born; now why the hell don't they leave me alone.

PRIVIE

Half a saltfish.

SEIGISMUNDO

But maybe that's what they did. They left me too much alone.

PRIVIE

A little barley.

SEIGISMUNDO

I am such a one as am too much alone.

PRIVIE

We could make a little beer with the barley, maybe.

SEIGISMUNDO

Is there any wine?

PRIVIE

No. No wine.

SEIGISMUNDO

Dammit. It's come to this.

PRIVIE

Do you want to divide the saltfish?

SEIGISMUNDO

No, we best save the best for a later occasion.

PRIVIE

What later?

SEIGISMUNDO

A later occasion.

PRIVIE

What occasion?

SEIGISMUNDO
Well, it may get worse than this.

PRIVIE
Oh, come on.

SEIGISMUNDO
Well, you never know.

PRIVIE
Yes, you do.

SEIGISMUNDO
(*Pause.*) You're right; let's eat the damn thing now.

(PRIVIE *breaks the fish in half. He then gives* SEIGISMUNDO *some walnuts.* SEIGISMUNDO *furtively attempts to break the shell with his teeth.* PRIVIE *sees his distress and breaks nuts and places them in* SEIGISMUNDO*'s mouth. The gesture is not a subservient one, but is done as if out of love.*)

SEIGISMUNDO
(*Pauses in his eating.*)
Why is this day different from all other days?

PRIVIE
It isn't; it's just closer.

SEIGISMUNDO
Oh.

PRIVIE
(*Speaking to himself.*)
I guess I could make some beer.

SEIGISMUNDO
What?

PRIVIE
I was saying . . .

SEIGISMUNDO

SEIGISMUNDO

You were saying what?

PRIVIE

I was saying I would make some beer.

SEIGISMUNDO

If what?

PRIVIE

If we had some water.

SEIGISMUNDO

But we don't have any water.

PRIVIE

Right; we don't have any water.

SEIGISMUNDO

How is it that we always have enough water to live?

PRIVIE

Oh, we always have enough to do that. And there will always be enough crumbs around to keep us eating (*pause*) —or at least alive.

SEIGISMUNDO

Yeah. There's always enough for that, dammit. It's all against us.

PRIVIE

No, it's not. It's worse. It doesn't even know we're here.

SEIGISMUNDO

What is it that keeps us going, then? Is it that the earth leads downward so that we fall forward? So that we always stay in motion?

PRIVIE

There's something crooked at the root of the world.

SEIGISMUNDO

Are you mocking me again?

PRIVIE

I don't think so.

SEIGISMUNDO

(*Pause.*) If only my mother . . .

PRIVIE

What! your mother again? I thought we agreed not to speak of that poor old hag in the dark anymore.

SEIGISMUNDO

If she hadn't gone rumping around the world. Rubbing up on this and that man for her sport.

PRIVIE

She only rubbed on one man.

SEIGISMUNDO

That was one too many.

PRIVIE
(*Laughing.*)

All but one shall live.

SEIGISMUNDO

You laugh on.

PRIVIE

Come on now; your mother hasn't had a damn thing to do with you for three score and ten years.

SEIGISMUNDO

A hell of a lot longer than that.

PRIVIE

Well, then she isn't responsible for you anymore.

SEIGISMUNDO

I'm supposed to accept that, eh?

PRIVIE

It's called maturity.

SEIGISMUNDO

Or senility. (*Pause.*) My tongue's swollen.

PRIVIE

So's mine.

SEIGISMUNDO

Mine was swollen yesterday.

PRIVIE

So, mine was too.

SEIGISMUNDO

What the hell do I care if your tongue's swollen, too. Is that supposed to make me feel better?

PRIVIE

Well, it's the best we can do.

SEIGISMUNDO

So?

PRIVIE

Well, do what you want to.

SEIGISMUNDO

I can't.

PRIVIE

Right; you can't.

SEIGISMUNDO

(*Pause.*) Why aren't you sad?

PRIVIE

I am sad.

SEIGISMUNDO

But you're not as sad as I am.

PRIVIE

That's because I'm crazy.

SEIGISMUNDO

Oh, that's right. I forgot. My memory is failing me, too.

PRIVIE

Not completely, though.

SEIGISMUNDO

True: not enough.

PRIVIE

Why don't you set up a charter of something?

SEIGISMUNDO

What kind of a charter could I possibly set up?

PRIVIE

A charter of grievances.

SEIGISMUNDO

A charter of grievances, indeed.

PRIVIE

It may do you some good.

SEIGISMUNDO

What could possibly do me any good?

PRIVIE

Say that you're displeased with the world.

SEIGISMUNDO

In such a place as this world is . . .

PRIVIE

Nothing can behoove a man . . .

SEIGISMUNDO

But to die . . .

PRIVIE

And assume the colors of the earth.

SEIGISMUNDO

(*Looking at him.*) What is that out there? Natura Naturata?

PRIVIE

No, just dead leaves.

SEIGISMUNDO

Oh.

PRIVIE

You can state in your charter what you want.

SEIGISMUNDO

What do I want?

PRIVIE

Your six feet of earth, of course.

SEIGISMUNDO

I wanted the world once.

PRIVIE

Yes, but now you'll settle for six feet of it.

SEIGISMUNDO

Yes, I'd be glad for that, I think.

PRIVIE

You'll get it sometime.

SEIGISMUNDO

Privie.

PRIVIE

Yes.

SEIGISMUNDO

(*Shyly.*) I have to go again.

PRIVIE

You just went a little while ago.

SEIGISMUNDO

I don't care when I went; I have to go again.

PRIVIE

Oh, you're a pest. What do you have to do: number one or number two?

SEIGISMUNDO

Number two, I think.

PRIVIE

(*Reaching into sack; takes out small green army surplus shovel.*) Here's the shovel.

SEIGISMUNDO

Have we any paper left?

PRIVIE

I think there's still a few pages from the Bible left. (*Takes out Bible; finds only the binder.*) No, I guess we used that all up. Get some leaves.

SEIGISMUNDO

Have I come to this state of ignominy?

PRIVIE

You can write it in your magna carta.

(Seigismundo *goes off with shovel to the back of stage and starts banging the shovel as if digging.*)

PRIVIE

It will be a good enough evening if it doesn't rain.

SEIGISMUNDO

What did you say?

PRIVIE

What?

SEIGISMUNDO

I said it will be all right if it doesn't rain.

SEIGISMUNDO

It never rains.

PRIVIE

I know.

(SEIGISMUNDO *goes back to digging.*)

PRIVIE

Of course, if it did rain I could put my feet in some cool water. (*Pause.*) However, if it doesn't rain, I won't get wet. Thank the Lord for whatever little blessings he gives us in spite of himself.

(SEIGISMUNDO *comes back wearily to* PRIVIE.)

PRIVIE

What's the matter?

SEIGISMUNDO

It's no good. I can't get anywhere.

PRIVIE

Oh, you are a pain.

SEIGISMUNDO

It doesn't matter.

PRIVIE

Why?

SEIGISMUNDO

I don't have to go anymore.

PRIVIE

You mean you're too damn lazy.

SEIGISMUNDO

All right, then I'm too lazy. If I had more food I wouldn't be so weak.

PRIVIE

If you had more food you'd just have to go more often.

SEIGISMUNDO

You're probably right. To think how many years I've spent perfecting a nervous system.

PRIVIE

I figure if we make camp here, we can make an energetic start in the morning.

SEIGISMUNDO

Well, we'll make some sort of departure in the morning. (*Pause.*) I have come upon a desert place yet familiar.

PRIVIE

Yes, it's a familiar enough place, Seigismundo.

SEIGISMUNDO

Have we everything we left with?

PRIVIE

More or less.

SEIGISMUNDO

Well, more or less?

PRIVIE

Surely less.

SEIGISMUNDO

Have we still the silver?

PRIVIE

(*Takes out silver tray.*) We have the little tray . . . and here are two pieces of silverware: a spoon and a misshapen fork.

SEIGISMUNDO

This is a sad state of affairs.

PRIVIE

No more so than usual. Here's a red piece of string. It probably belonged to your uniform.

SEIGISMUNDO

Let me see that. (*Snatches it from* Privie's *hand.*) Dammit, you could have taken better care.

PRIVIE

What better care could I have taken?

SEIGISMUNDO

(*Staring at string.*) God, but it seems like a long time ago.

PRIVIE

Time passes more or less.

SEIGISMUNDO

A while ago this was a cause for praise.

PRIVIE

Weren't you the grand fellow then?

SEIGISMUNDO

Don't speak of it so lightly: there were many who followed.

PRIVIE

You looked good in the old thing, though.

SEIGISMUNDO

I had a body for it then.

PRIVIE

Straight as an arrow, with a nice round ass for sitting on horses and in coaches.

SEIGISMUNDO

A more dignified means of locomotion, certainly.

PRIVIE

And the women were moved for you.

SEIGISMUNDO

There were some who were moved. (*Pause.*) There were even some among them who loved me.

PRIVIE

Loved you. (*Laughing.*) Come on now.

SEIGISMUNDO

No, really. There were some. Some who walked with me past the cobbled streets.

PRIVIE

And the rain.

SEIGISMUNDO

And some past the rain and the yellowing leaves.

PRIVIE

And even some to the harbor.

SEIGISMUNDO

Past the ships and the dead soldiers. And the stars which are fingers of God. So many women. So many girls.

PRIVIE

And you say some of these loved you.

SEIGISMUNDO

And me jumping in and out of their thighs, the watering thighs and the screaming beds.

PRIVIE

You were a hell of a fellow then, eh?

SEIGISMUNDO

Oh, they wanted it so badly. (*Pause.*) I wonder how I ever had the strength to please them all. In and out, in and out like that.

PRIVIE

You used more energy on the women than you ever used in battle.

SEIGISMUNDO

I like the desperation of love. (*Pause.*) Pity, I've fallen out of the habit. Why don't you do a little dance for me or something?

PRIVIE

I'm not up to any more dances. You'll have to amuse yourself from now on.

SEIGISMUNDO

So you won't even dance for me anymore? Won't even give me a bit of merriment to ease me?

PRIVIE

You can dance for yourself.

SEIGISMUNDO

You know I can't.

PRIVIE

Just lift one leg before another.

SEIGISMUNDO

I'd look like an old fowl struck by lightning.

PRIVIE

No, you'd look like an old man dancing.

SEIGISMUNDO

There was one girl in especial. I can't remember her name or her face.

PRIVIE

Call her Margret; it doesn't matter.

SEIGISMUNDO

Yes, this one girl, Margret.

PRIVIE

Who was prettier than most.

SEIGISMUNDO

Who was different from most. She made me come in her handkerchief so she could always keep my smell, she said.

PRIVIE

Wonder what happened to that kerchief.

SEIGISMUNDO

It passed to the waters as she must have. Everything returns to water. (*Pause.*) I wish I knew about death.

Knew what?

SEIGISMUNDO

Knew what guise she would come in.

PRIVIE

Why?

SEIGISMUNDO

So that she would not pass me without my knowing. Then I could give up a last fart and die.

PRIVIE

Oh, you'll know her when she comes.

(*There is a pause wherein* SEIGISMUNDO *sits down and plays with the bell of his tricycle. He rings bell three times and* PRIVIE *offers him a fig in a mock-mass gesture, placing the fig in his mouth.*)

SEIGISMUNDO

Strange that I should have chanced to find you here among this tangle of broken images.

PRIVIE

You didn't chance to find me; you sought me out.

SEIGISMUNDO

And did I find you one weary day after I invented the wheel?

PRIVIE

I invented the wheel.

SEIGISMUNDO

Really? Are you sure?

PRIVIE

Yes.

SEIGISMUNDO

Perhaps you're right.

PRIVIE

I invented the wheel and you used it.

SEIGISMUNDO

If you were kind, you'd end it for me. It wouldn't cause you much labor. You could sort of fall on me with your crutches. I don't have very much wind left in me.

PRIVIE

If I were to do that who would bury me?

SEIGISMUNDO

What the hell does it matter if anybody buries you?

PRIVIE

Who do you think you are that I should make your death for you?

SEIGISMUNDO

I'm one who, between the dark hour and the hour of light, has found himself concerned.

PRIVIE

If you're concerned it's only for yourself.

SEIGISMUNDO

And who else should I weep for but myself? Who is more worthy of pity? Sitting here as I am, staring into the void.

PRIVIE

Ha ha, the void.

SEIGISMUNDO

Why are you laughing?

PRIVIE

There ain't no void.

SEIGISMUNDO

What is the cretin smile I see on the face of the night?

PRIVIE

No face.

SEIGISMUNDO

The void is the halfway house between the upward and the downward.

PRIVIE

There is no upper or lower.

SEIGISMUNDO

Then what is this sadness I feel?

PRIVIE

The sadness is because there is no terror. Because there is no void. And nothing which pursues you or conspires against you.

SEIGISMUNDO

Nothing?

PRIVIE

Nothing before you and nothing behind you.

SEIGISMUNDO

This too makes me tragic.

PRIVIE

You can't be tragic; you haven't the ability.

SEIGISMUNDO

Don't tell me that I'm not tragic.

PRIVIE

Nothing tragic about you.

SEIGISMUNDO

(*Crazed, with anger.*) Look at me here. How I've suffered. How I've felt so much.

PRIVIE

Oh, you try but I've not been put off by your devices.

SEIGISMUNDO

I didn't want to be born.

PRIVIE

I didn't want to be born, either.

SEIGISMUNDO

But there was more passion in your birth than mine.

PRIVIE

More accident than passion.

SEIGISMUNDO

What have I if I have no sorrow?

PRIVIE

You have your devices.

SEIGISMUNDO

Is that all?

PRIVIE

All?

SEIGISMUNDO

My face has altered.

PRIVIE

Yes.

SEIGISMUNDO

My hands have altered.

PRIVIE

Yes.

SEIGISMUNDO

What can be worse than these things?

PRIVIE

To do those things without grandeur. To have done everything to no end.

SEIGISMUNDO

But what of the things I feel so intensely, the things which set me apart?

PRIVIE

A matter of occasion only.

SEIGISMUNDO

How many ways can I say that I want to die?

PRIVIE

You don't want to die. Why don't you stop all this?

SEIGISMUNDO

But I'm serious about it all.

PRIVIE

So are children. Children are so serious that they kill you.

SEIGISMUNDO

And you sit there with your calm provincial face and call me a liar.

PRIVIE

Your devices are a lie.

SEIGISMUNDO

You're a very clever fellow.

PRIVIE

Oh.

SEIGISMUNDO

You see everything, don't you?

PRIVIE

No, just too much.

SEIGISMUNDO

That's why I like you, I think. For your mind.

PRIVIE

You hate me for my mind.

SEIGISMUNDO

No, I like you, really.

PRIVIE

There's no way in the world you could possibly like me; I know too much.

SEIGISMUNDO

(*Picking up tricycle and moving behind the seated figure of* PRIVIE.) You really should be more trusting. (*Strikes* PRIVIE *three times with tricycle.*) There now. That will put an end to your crying. So you know what all of my devices are. Ungrateful bastard! Better to be alone than suffer this mockery. I'll weep at the moon for myself then. (*He climbs on tricycle, starts to go, thinks again, and changes direction such that he goes off in the same direction from which he came. Leaves buskins behind on stage with the body of* PRIVIE.)

Ring bell.

Darkness.

Claudia

He seemed suspended, hanging in front of the drugstore. His head dipped, then jerked erect. One spin-
dled arm supported his lurching body, its fingers
splayed like taeniae against the display window. His
other hand clasped a can of malt liquor behind his
back. Stoned, he appeared intent on going through
the glass. He pressed his face against it; his features
flattening into a grotesque, black mask. Opening a
toothless smile, he studied the various ads for headache remedies, hair straighteners, black culture meetings, laxatives, jazz concerts, revival meetings and
skin lighteners. He laughed, pulled back and slapped
his thigh—stumbling sideways with the impact. The
can rose spasmodically to his face, and he gulped at
it. He gagged, coughed, then wiped at the ring of
white foam about his mouth. "Right on, brother,"
someone said, and he turned. Cursing and gesturing,
he staggered into the street and, defying Lenox
Avenue's rush-hour traffic, made his way downtown
along the middle of the southbound traffic lane.

Inside the store, the owner, Vernon Daubs, sat behind a counter near the door. He watched the drunk,
mumbled "crazy nigger" and continued fanning himself with a folded newspaper.

Further back, at the rear of the store, Claudia
Williams stood behind a small luncheonette counter.

FRANKLIN JACKSON

It was nearly closing time, and she leaned forward, resting against the glass pastry shelf that stretched half the length of the counter. She was attractive. The white uniform contrasted with her coffee color and her smooth skin gave her face a youthful look. It was only her darkly circled eyes that belied that first impression. Still, with her slim build, she might easily have been mistaken for a teen-ager.

Weary from the past eight hours, her face was set in an expression of fatigued calm. But her eyes moved restlessly between the clock across from her and the glass doors up front. The few customers who came into the store smiled and stared awkwardly. She ignored them until Tommy Jackson pushed through the doors.

Tommy was heavy, dark-complexioned, but he moved agilely, with a stiff-legged, bouncing stride. A thick growth of hair encircled his chin. Walking quickly past Mr. Daubs, he smiled confidently and, with his forearms, hitched his soiled khakis up onto his hips.

"What's happening, pops," he said, glancing back at the old man.

Mr. Daubs frowned and drew on his cigar as Tom threw himself noisily onto one of the stools in front of the counter.

Claudia glanced at him, then at the clock. Her mouth twisted into a disdainful grimace. At the same time she raised her chin and lifted her shoulder, bracing herself. The uniform stretched tightly across her body with the effort and, noticing Tom's eyes moving over her, she tried to relax.

"Baby, can a hungry cat like me cop somethin' back here?" he asked.

He laughed and flashed a smile.

Claudia pushed her hand through the soft, reddish hair that framed her face, and turned toward him.

"It's closing time, sweety, you know that as well as I do."

"I don't want no grits, baby. You know what I mean. What you doin' after work tonight?"

"Haven't you caught on yet—you're a drag, dear. Why don't you go rap to somebody who wants to hear it."

Tommy laughed and pushed himself back onto the stool. In front, Mr. Daubs turned and stared back toward the luncheonette. He bit down viciously on his cigar and frowned. The skin on his forehead fell into four, deep, evenly spaced furrows.

"Why the hell are you so damn loud and repulsive," Claudia snapped. "There's nothing happening here, baby, nothing. You ought to just split and make everybody happy."

"Come on off it, sugar, you don't have to go through all those changes with me. We both know where you're at." He paused, his head cocked and his face broadened with a smile. "Why don't you straighten up and come on in, we could git into somethin' mellow."

Claudia moved to the sink beneath the counter and began rinsing the remainder of the dirty glasses. She raised her eyes and stared at him.

"Look, boy! You don't have a chance. You can't pay for it and you damn sure can't get it any other way, so forget it."

"Aw right," he said, "but I ain't gonna be around always, baby, you better quit being so damned uppity and come down to earth." He turned and walked away, his arms swinging stiffly at his sides. At the doors, he stopped and shouted back to her: "You still lookin' good, baby, and I ain't givin' up yet. 'Scuse me, pops, I didn't mean to disturb you," he said, as he glanced at Mr. Daubs. Laughing, he pushed through the doors and disappeared into the crowd outside.

Claudia looked up at the clock. It was six and time to quit. In a few minutes she stood in front of Mr. Daubs with a thin sweater thrown over her shoulders.

"I'll see you next week," she said.

Daubs dropped his cigar on the floor. "See if you can't keep them hoodlums outta here if you wantta keep this job," he mumbled. "And be on time Monday."

"Sure, Mr. Daubs," she answered.

Outside, she walked quickly up Lenox Avenue, toward 145th Street. The drugstore was only a few blocks from her apartment, but the walk along Lenox annoyed her. Her eyes moved from the curb to the row of buildings at her right and, without changing her expression, she laughed to herself. It reminded her of a scene in a movie she had watched —when the Indians made Kirk Douglas run the gauntlet. The same faces stared at her from the steps of broken-down tenements or the windows of poolhalls and bars. The same voices called to her from groups of teen-agers and old men huddled about parking meters or leaning against the fenders of parked cars, and the same lean, heavy-eyed young men accidentally bumped into her and tried to strike up a conversation. Someday, she told herself, she'd figure out a way to keep these mothers off her back. For now, there was only one thing to do—ignore them. Pushing her head back and staring straight ahead, she quickened her pace. At 144th Street, she turned and walked toward Seventh Avenue.

The street was lined on either side by rows of squat, three-story stone buildings. In the twilight they were fused together, a thick, monotonous wall. From the windows, behind gray curtains, the faces of wrinkled men and women could be seen. They watched their grandchildren playing amid the scattered newspapers and debris that covered the streets; watched their children sitting on stoops or listened to their angry voices as they stood in boisterous groups at the corner or huddled in dark doorways; watched the crap and poker games across the street in front of the store-front church; listened to the sound of a child crying below them and watched the young woman in the white uniform and sweater as she walked quickly past their windows and disappeared inside one of the arched doorways that led through dark, narrow hallways to pinched rooms exactly like their own. They watched, pressed their knotted fingers together, and, hope having dissolved in the heat and fatigue of summers long passed and scarcely remembered, sank back down into their reveries.

In her apartment, Claudia lay across a daybed—a thin robe wrapped tightly around herself. She had cooked and eaten, and now, exhausted, listened to the pleading blues that sounded from her phonograph. The singer's voice sank, cracked, broke, then effortlessly rose and settled in a smooth, lusty tone, drawing out the last words of the lyrics. Claudia listened and felt tears gathering in her eyes. She struggled with herself, fighting her emotions, but finally relented and buried her face in the pillow.

It was crazy; she knew it. Crying didn't help anything, and yet, since the accident, when she left Newark and came to New York, the tears had become familiar to her. Once she had fought the urge, telling herself it was only weakness and self-pity and that tears, like sex, meant nothing in Harlem. It worked for a time, and she had felt reconciled to her life, despite its shortcomings. But her resistance, like cheap shoes, had worn quickly.

The phonograph rejected and the record began again. She thought of Newark and her parents—wondered how things might have been had they lived.

Dreaming, always dreaming. She wiped her eyes with the collar of her robe. Taking a washcloth from her bureau and picking up the box of cleanser from the kitchen sink, she cracked the door to the apartment and glanced down the darkened hallway. Mr. Bronson's door was still open. She could see the shaft of light that lay between her and the door to the bathroom at the other end of the hallway. She closed the door and straightened her robe before stepping back into the hallway. Passing Mr. Bronson's room, she sensed his eyes on her and felt a self-gratifying contempt.

After washing the tub and turning on the hot water, she started back to her room. Mr. Bronson took the wine bottle away from his mouth long enough to mumble some obscenity. Claudia ignored him. She paused and considered stopping across the hall at Sylvia's apartment when she saw the glow of a light beneath the door. Stepping closer and hearing the sound of a man's laughter inside, she changed her mind. Sylvia wouldn't want visitors. She went back into her apartment, poured herself a drink and lay back down on the bed.

She gazed about her, then closed her eyes. She hated the apartment. There was only one room and after six years it was still practically bare. The few things she had were rundown and falling apart. A few pieces of furniture, a phonograph, some records and a shelf of old dusty books, that's all she had to show for all those years on her own. And she had intended to have so much. That's why she had denied herself. Now it seemed as if she'd always been denying herself. For this, for nothing.

All those years, after she came to live with her aunt in Harlem, she'd denied herself. She had needed so much, and nothing was given unless there was a trick to it. Claudia laughed. Her aunt had tried. She was a good woman, a good mother to her children, but she worked hard to support her family and had little time for an intruder. The rest, the children, her aunt's husband, they had made the apartment more of a nightmare than the street. It was only her dreams that kept her going, kept her from getting down and wallowing with the others—the ones her mother had called low niggers. She had held herself aloof, avoided the dark parties, the easy friendships and quick hugs. She studied, dreamed and tried to save herself for something better. But nothing had turned out right. It couldn't have been worse if she had just let herself go; even the whores on 114th Street lived better than she did. She finished the drink and got up. She must've been crazy—dreaming, thinking she could keep herself above the shit. All that time, and not once had anything come of it.

Moving to the dresser, she picked up a small hand mirror. The cockroach that sat beneath it remained still for an instant, then shot toward the crevice between the dresser and the wall. Her free hand came down on it like a hammer. She wiped up the remains with a tissue and tossed it into the bag of garbage near the sink. After rinsing her hands, she took the mirror, a shower cap and a hairbrush and, sitting down at the table, began pinning her hair up.

Only once, with Hal Fletcher, had she even thought there was a chance of fulfillment. She met him at a dance in the Bronx a few months after she left her aunt and began living alone. He was tall and impeccably dressed, and the boyish smile, which seemed permanently etched into his face, set him apart from the others. At first she had thought he was shy and, trying to avoid the pressure of slow grinds, glib lines and fast talk, she sought him out. She was surprised to find him neither as young nor as shy as she had expected. Yet, from the moment they spoke to each other, she trusted him. He was soft-spoken and his manners had the gloss of refinement. Like herself, he seemed aloof, uninvolved with the sweat and strain of the nitty-gritty; and she took his aloofness as evidence of his sharing her aspirations as well as her denial of the others' vulgarity.

Even now she swore that he hadn't tried to hit on her that first night; but somehow the music, the heat, the liquor and his apparent indifference disarmed her. She loosened the reins that had held her desires in check. Unleashed, they ran rampant and, when the sprint ended, she lay, tired and perspiring, in his bed.

She was no virgin, her aunt's husband Charles had long ago come crawling out of an after-hours joint stinking of cheap whiskey and, as he said, put the thing to her good. But this was the first time she had given herself to a man of her own accord. She didn't regret it then, but afterward, when it was too late, she realized it had been desperation, the hope of filling that corner of her dream set off for the right man. And still later, that hope, as much as Hal's honey-voiced pledges of his affection, led her to drop the reins completely. She threw herself into the affair, convinced this was the chance she had waited for, this was her man.

It lasted for almost three months.

They saw each other almost every day at first. She worked in a restaurant in Brooklyn and, at a quarter of four each day, she would begin watching the front window for Hal's car. She never knew if he was coming. He told her that whenever he got away from work early enough he would come by for her. Most days he drove up, blew the horn and sat waiting until four when she was off.

"Madam, do you know you're a fox," he would say when she came out. Flashing a broad smile, he would step out onto the sidewalk and usher her into his Cadillac as if it were a royal chariot.

Holding back the urge to laugh, she would push her nose into the air, pull her skirt up, and step daintily into the car. "Home, James," she'd say. After he scurried around to the driver's seat, they would both break up and fall into each other's arms laughing.

"Soon, baby, you won't have to work in that joint," he told her once, as they started for her apartment. Later he teased her: "You laugh and pretend it's funny, but I can tell, sugar, underneath you dig that 'Home, James' bit. Don't you?"

At this she puffed her face up with mock indignation and leaned away from him, waiting for his arm to slide along the back of the seat and draw her close again. When he did, she rested her head against his chest and, holding him tightly, let her eyes stray to the faces of the people they passed. She was proud of Hal, and, when she noticed someone staring at them, her pride would swell even more. She would reach up and kiss him or let her hand run playfully along his thigh. And at those moments, she was sure that he too was proud.

Later, at her apartment, he would usually park and walk her to the door. Sometimes he went inside and, while he listened to one of the albums he had brought when he began seeing her, she cooked. He loved her cooking and always complimented her:

"Girl, the way you cook, you must be some kin to Aunt Jemima."

"If nothing else," she laughed, "my aunt did teach me how to make a good pot of greens."

After eating, they would lie on the daybed and drink until she fell asleep. On the mornings after, she awoke finding herself alone, undressed and tucked beneath the covers.

A few times, on Fridays, instead of parking and walking her to the door, he told her to pack some things and spend the weekend with him. She never refused. Driving from Harlem to Queens, for her, was like moving closer to her dream. She realized it was foolish, but each time they left the cramped tenements and restless crowds she imagined herself escaping a concentration camp. Her room, her street was a besieged area, upon whose blistered, sterile grounds the seeds of her dreams had fallen and almost expired. And now it was Hal who opened the gates and, freeing her, allowed those seeds to be sown on richer soil. She felt closer to him, more dependent upon him then, than at any other time. He was her hope, her savior, come to lead her to the promised land. His was a different world—the vaguely remembered world of Newark and childhood, the world she had seen on movie and television screens, spacious, full of fine clothes, expensive things—as far from Harlem as heaven from hell.

He lived in Forest Hills and, when they drove up to the complex of high-rise buildings, he parked the car and they always went to the supermarket across the street. When they had gotten the groceries to his apartment, she unpacked them while he made drinks.

"No wonder you so skinny, sugar," she said, "there's never any food here until I come. What do you do when I'm not here?"

Coming up behind her, he put his arms around her waist and, moving his hips against her, whispered in her ear:

"I honestly don't know how I make it, baby, but it's a groove when you're here, you dig."

"Fool, get on out of here," she laughed and, turning around, pushed him toward the door.

After starting to cook, she went about cleaning and straightening up the apartment. Sometimes, when the food was almost ready and the odor of black-eyed peas and rice —his favorite dish—hung rich and heavy in the air, she went out onto the terrace.

The apartment was on the sixteenth floor and she could see for miles. Across from her the rush-hour traffic crawled reluctantly along the expressway. Beyond that, as far as she could see, streamlined buildings with steel and glass that sparkled in the evening sun pushed upward toward the sky. Her eyes wandered and, overwhelmed by the vastness that confronted her, she leaned back against the sliding glass doors, feeling small and unbearably weak. Within, beneath the maze of impulses that moved her from day to day, a feeling, a warmth, would rise up; and, when she could no longer deny the truth of that feeling, when she knew that to be there with Hal, always, was all that she wanted, she would slowly shake her head and tell herself yes, this is where it is.

Inside the apartment, within the comfort of Hal's arms, she had sought the words to tell him how she felt, but never found them. He would laugh, asking why she was acting so serious. Pushing her head against his neck and shoulder, she would always say it was nothing and promise herself that later, at the right moment, she'd tell him. But later, after they had eaten and gone to one of the nightclubs in Corona or Jamaica, they would fall, exhausted, into bed and, with the heat of his body pressed against her, somehow words, questions, no matter how important they may have been before, seemed unnecessary.

On Saturdays they stayed at the apartment until late afternoon. Hal watched a baseball game or prizefight on television, and Claudia busied herself in another room. She particularly enjoyed looking through the shelves of books that covered one wall of the living room. She had still hoped to enroll in night school at City College and, at that time, read as much as possible. Often during an afternoon, she finished a book and, later, when she and Hal walked along the winding pathways that connected the buildings, she would question him about it. Since she had never seen him reading, it always surprised her that he was able to answer her questions without hesitation.

He told her once that he had taken a number of sociology courses and remembered most of the books they had used.

When she asked why he'd studied sociology if he had intended to go into business, he'd turned and, looking down at her with a smug expression, laughed softly.

"There's something I have to hip you to, baby," he said, as he led her to one of the benches that lined the pathway. "You know, I grew up in the same neighborhood you live in now. Niggers sweeping floors and cleaning toilets during the week, drinking and cutting each other on weekends. My little sister was out on the street screwing at twelve. Yeah, she was making it with a cat I used to play handball with— when I found out, I used to kick his ass every time I saw him." Crossing his legs, he brushed some lint from the cuff of his pants. "He had a sister too. I think she was about fifteen then. And a few weeks before I left for college, I got to her. I picked her up at a party, bought some wine and took her to a friend's apartment. Me and three of my buddies pulled a train on her, kept her there all night, then put her out the next morning.

"That shocks you, doesn't it?" he said, and he placed his hand on top of hers. She was trembling. "That's one difference between you and me, baby—you sailed over the shit and I had to crawl right through it. But you learn something when you down there, and when or if you ever get out, things are much clearer. I was one of the lucky ones, I got out. After my father left, Mom hit the numbers, big. That's how I got to college." He grinned and put his arm around her shoulder. "If those rich, yellow, bourgeois bitches in D.C. had known they was dating a poor nigger from Harlem they would've died.

"Anyway, when I got there, I was curious, like you; I wanted to know why Whitey had and we didn't. Sociology seemed like the best way to find out. And it didn't take long, despite the efforts of some of them Tom professors." He took out his cigarettes, lit two, and handed one to Claudia. "You know, when I was down there in Harlem, living with it every day, nobody could've convinced me that the whole situation was really our fault. I was mad, angry, baby, like the cats raising so much hell now—ready to go up side Whitey's head anytime I got a chance. I was stupid, you dig."

"You're talking like one of them crackers," Claudia said. "You don't really believe we're responsible for what's going on."

"Well no, we certainly wasn't responsible for being put into this mess. But getting out, that's something else. Here, let me run it down to you.

"The real difference between Whitey and us is actually simple, baby—we feel more. They pretend they feel more than we do, even accuse us of being savages, brutes, am I right? But they know for a fact that practically every member feels more than they do. All you have to do is look at the religions to see what I mean. Our people go to church and, dig it, swear they feel the Holy spirit; when it gets to them, it's so real it moves them physically. Might even move their bowels. And if they don't feel the spirit, they sure as hell feel the fear of God. But how many nonmembers have you heard talking about feeling the spirit, or, for that matter, actually feeling anything. None baby. They don't feel it inside. It comes in up here." He tapped his forehead. "They discipline themselves, set up rules which they follow when it's practical. But, if it's necessary to break a rule, it's no big thing because they don't feel it."

Claudia nodded her head in agreement.

"Well, that's how they want it, and that's just why most of us don't get anywhere. They talk about morality and we listen, then bust our asses trying to do what's right. And, while we're feeling the spirit, shrinking from the wrath of God, sitting in or marching for freedom and equality, and talking about soul, you know what they're doing—making money. Gettin' that dough. It's as simple as that. All of us do the same things, make the same mistakes, but, when we're finished, we're uptight, sitting at home with an empty stomach and a room full of rats, feeling evil. Meanwhile, they're out here living it up, enjoying the good things, maybe feeling a little high from some good Scotch. And the thing is, they're right.

"That's all I meant when I said we're responsible for the situation. All we have to do, if we want to improve things, is control them feelings. That goes for everybody—the ones begging and talking about nonviolence and the ones screaming about power and black arts and trying to tear up everything they don't have. Soul, passion or whatever you want to call it, it's all right up to a point. But it don't put no beans on the table. The Man doesn't understand it. It scares him and, after all, he's got the money. Besides, feeling, conviction, that ain't no match for calculation. If we want to make it, we have to start thinking, be a little pragmatic. Dig on what's his name . . . Willie James. Do what's necessary to get what you want, even if you feel like it might not be right—that's the only way to have anything. As soon as we learn that, we'll get all the equality we need."

Taking his arm away from her shoulder, Hal placed a cigarette between his lips and, standing up, searched the pockets of his jacket for his lighter.

"Anyway, when I discovered how things were, I decided that the business world was for me," he said, as he lit the cigarette. "You see what I mean?"

"Yes, I think so," she said. She still wasn't sure that she really did. Standing, she took his arm and they started back to the apartment. What she was sure of was that Hal had made it; he had done exactly what she dreamed of doing. Wrapping both of her arms about his, she smiled and pressed her face against the sleeve of his jacket.

"You know, you're a fairly smart chick," he said, as they stepped into the elevator. He grinned. "I think things are going to work out fine."

Later, they went to a restaurant on Northern Boulevard and, from there, to a jazz club in Manhattan's East Sixties. It was nearly dawn when they drove back toward his apartment. The expressway was deserted and a faint orange glow had just appeared on the horizon. Claudia leaned against the door of the car. With the soft sound of a jazz ballad drifting from the tape recorder, she moved her foot along his calf and watched as he turned toward her and smiled. She felt good and, as the car pulled to a halt in front of his apartment, she suppressed an urge to giggle and throw herself into his arms; instead, she waited and, when he had gotten out of the car and opened the door on her side, she stepped quietly from the car and pressed her body against his.

She had enjoyed those weekends, but they were as rare as the cool breeze that occasionally cut through the summer's sucking heat and flowed into her room. Usually Hal had neither asked her to come with him nor come inside with her. After picking her up at work, he walked her to her door and stopped. While they talked he would lean against one of the huge decorative columns that sat on each side of the door. When he finished smoking, he would kiss her lightly on the cheek, at the same time patting her behind, and tell her he had to split if they wanted to keep on living in high-style. Although she had considered it, she never asked him to stay. Instead she forced a smile and watched as he returned to the car, straightened his jacket and tie, and drove off. When the car moved onto Lenox Avenue and out of sight, she went inside and spent the rest of the evening reading and hoping she'd see him the next day.

She wondered, after it was all over, how she had let herself become so deeply involved, and she had to laugh. After the first night he was probably out there telling all the slicks how he had stroked this lame chick the first time he met her. Even though he had sworn that he loved her and, for the first time, made her feel that making something of herself was worthwhile, he had never really said anything about the future. He had even been reluctant to commit himself for the next day. She should have known no good would come of it—that was the thing that got to her. When she thought about it, Hal's lying was really not that much of a surprise to her; she wouldn't have put that past any brother. It was the way she had convinced herself that he was on the square, like some silly white bitch, that hurt her. It seemed incredible that she had sat back, like a dog, waiting for him to call. But she had, and, though she bitterly denied it later, she had enjoyed it.

It was only during the last few weeks, when Hal began calling less frequently, that her doubt grew. In his absence, suspicion was a chill, and she struggled to insulate her dreams. He had said that he worked for a company down-town, but despite her questioning, he always avoided telling her where he worked or what he did. Still, when they were together, money flowed like water. Uptown, wherever they went, everyone seemed to know him; they even recognized his car. She asked about it, but he avoided answering. Seeing that the questions annoyed him, she stopped asking; but alone she wondered and, sometimes, was convinced he was lying. Even so, she never pressed him. Not until the last night did she lose faith, and then only when her dream had been ripped apart.

She hadn't seen or heard from him in more than a week when she called his apartment. He had warned her never to call him at home, since he was usually busy and didn't want to be disturbed, but he hadn't been upset when he answered the phone. He told her he would see her later that evening.

It was Sunday, and for a short time, she sat in front of the window as somber-faced sisters and brothers clad in their best attire filed out of the church and, reluctant to make their way home, stood on the sidewalk gossiping and rehashing the sermon. Later, anticipation sent her pacing nervously about the room. She realized she was acting like a child, and she had to get a hold of herself.

When Hal arrived, she was still tense, but he didn't seem to notice. At the door, he kissed her, then quickly moved to the table and sat down. She had already cooked and, soon, they sat opposite each other eating. During dinner, he was unusually quiet. Only once, when he smiled and said something about soul food putting meat on your ribs, did he seem himself. Afterward, he sat on the daybed tapping his foot in time with the sound of a recording and staring at the ceiling. Claudia stood at the sink washing dishes.

Since she had hoped he wouldn't see how his absence had upset her, she had been relieved when her uneasiness went unnoticed. But now she was worried. Something was bothering him, and she wasn't sure what it was. She lifted the stopper from the sink and watched as the water, gray and greasy, spun through the drain with a loud gurgling noise. When she turned, he was still staring toward the ceiling. She poured two drinks and, after setting one of them on the chair at the end of the daybed, sat down at the table and looked out at the lighted windows of the buildings across the street. Moments later, when she turned back toward him, Hal was peering toward her over the rim of his glass. She moved to the sink and pulled the top from the fifth of bourbon.

"Is something wrong?" she asked.

He didn't answer. The light switch clicked and the room was black except for the glow of the streetlight outside the window. In a moment his body was against hers and his lips danced over the back of her neck.

"I'm sorry, baby," he said. He slipped his arm around her waist and pulled her against him. "I missed you. I wanted to see you but I couldn't. I hope I didn't worry you too much."

She turned and pressed her face against his chest. Her hands moved along his back.

"Hal, I was so scared. I . . . I thought you'd left me. I love you, more than anything, more than myself."

"I know, baby," he whispered. He kissed her. "I know. But don't worry now, it's going to be all right."

His arm slid down to the back of her knees and, still whispering, he picked her up and carried her to the daybed. He undressed her slowly, talking to her all the while, and when his body came down onto hers, she closed her eyes, shutting out the tears.

Later, he lay on his stomach with one arm hanging over the edge of the bed. She pressed herself against him, moving her mouth against his shoulder. Her teeth scraped his skin and she laughed softly.

"I needed you, baby," she said, and she couldn't suppress the inexplicable giggle that came to her throat. She moved closer.

He turned toward her and smiled. Her hands, cupped and accepting, moved toward his face, but he stood up. He padded to the phonograph and turned the record over. A ballad began with a long trumpet solo; it enveloped the room, a dirge, and Claudia clasped her hands together. Hal returned—sat on the side of the bed, silent and distant. She caressed his back.

"What's the matter, baby?" she asked. "We can talk about it."

He studied her. His lips were drawn tight across his teeth and his eyes were cold, analytical. He closed them, shutting out her gaze. His fingers glided along the soft down on her arm and he turned toward the window.

"Money, baby, that's what's wrong," he said. He shrugged his shoulders and his fingers moved upward along her arm.

"And I thought I was so damn smart. Thought I had everything under control."

"It doesn't matter, Hal, you still have your job. You'll straighten things out."

"That's just it, I don't have a job."

"But Hal, what happened?"

He swung his legs onto the bed and lay on his back sucking at his cigarette; his other hand moving over Claudia's body.

"I didn't tell you, baby, but I never had a job, as such, just investments."

"Why didn't . . ."

"Look, maybe I should have told you, but it doesn't matter now. It's too late. I blew. Everything is gone."

He moved to his side and, stretching his arm to the chair at the head of the bed, butted his cigarette in the ashtray.

"The thing is, sugar, until I get myself back together, I don't think I'll be able to see you," he said.

Instinctively, she moved closer to him; her hands clinging to his back, she pressed her face against his shoulder. For moments neither of them spoke. From the phonograph a piano weaved a quiet melody over the rhythm of bass and drums and, outside, a police siren shut out the clamor of laughter and shouting from the sidewalk.

"Hal, I can help," she said. "I have a little money saved and I still have my job."

He encircled her head with his arm and, pulling her closer, softly kissed her forehead. And she waited, a child now, for his words.

"I don't want to take your money. You don't even have enough for yourself," he said. He kissed her again and she felt her skin tingling as his hand moved slowly over her body. "There is a way though, but baby—I don't know if you're ready for it."

He paused and kissed her hair. She was trembling and her fingers dug into his back. Her mind succumbed and she slipped down—down into her body. She moaned as he moved his hips against her.

"You know I'll do anything for you, Hal, as long as we're

together." Her lips touched his. "As long as you're here and I can touch you . . ."

His fingers moved along her cheek, then, still holding her, he pulled back.

"Tell me, sugar, what is it?" she asked.

"Well, I have a friend, downtown, and . . . well, when I talked to him last week, he said he had a position open. He could give you a chance to make some real money. And with the kind of paper you'd make down there we wouldn't have no problems." He stared at her from what seemed like a great distance; her eyes were closed and she breathed heavily in his arms. Leaning closer, he brushed his lips against her neck and breasts. "Everything would be together, just like it was before. We could have everything we wanted and, soon, I'd be back on my feet again."

"What would I have to do?"

Her voice cracked and he felt her body stiffen under his hands. He moved his lips to her ear. His voice was softer now, tender and hypnotically reassuring. When he spoke, the words were hardly audible.

"You won't have to do much, sugar—just act as hostess. Be smart, and be nice to a few friends of ours. There's nothing to worry about . . ."

And he continued, but she didn't hear a word. A moment's disbelief, then her body tightened, as if the air was sucked from the room. She was suffocating. She struggled to shut out the voice, strange now, slithering in the darkness. She felt hands, cold on her skin, and pushed them away. Her face twisted with pain; she pressed herself against the wall. Her head moved convulsively from side to side and she gripped the wooden support under the bed. Her body shook with silent, epileptic sobs. Again, the hands, like worms, moving over her, pulling her toward him. The voice whispering, urging, soft, warm and moist on her neck. He pulled her back. Turned around, she was locked against him. She felt him, moving against the sweat of her breasts and thighs —felt his manhood rearing against her. Her body heaved under his fingers. "I need you," came to her throat, and she gagged—disgusted. "God! Oh God no!" she moaned, and pulled away. She crawled from the bed, stumbling in the darkness, feeling her way across the room.

She never knew what enabled her to rise and push the light switch; what strengthened her when she turned, her face rigid, her eyes closed, and told him to leave. But somehow she stood naked beneath the stark light, trembling, waiting for him to dress.

"You're a fool, baby," he said, standing in the doorway. His lips still curled in an innocent grin. "Whitey got your mind messed up now, but you'll learn. You'll need me again, momma, don't forget it."

She slammed the door, and, her hands at her temples, leaned against it. She stared across the room, at the bed and the glasses and her clothes scattered about the floor. For a moment, the room, everything in it, seemed incredibly calm; but she could sense it coming alive, vibrating—and inside, she felt the pain, swelling, growing. She pressed her head back against the door and clenched her fist against her cheek. She sobbed and her body was shaken by a cold chill that cut into her like an axe and left her limp on the floor. Her hand pounded methodically against the door and she cursed silently, beneath her breath. Finally, her voice lifted in an obscene cry and she gasped for breath.

Never. Never again, she told herself. They wanted to use her, have her, if possible, sell her. Well, now she knew. No more. She was a fool. She trusted them—Charles and Hal, but no more. No more dreams, no more bullshit. "No more," she said, and she bit down on her lip and tried to hold back the tears. Her head dropped, and she lay there throughout the night.

Her hair rolled into tight curls now, Claudia stood up, put the mirror back on the dresser and pulled the shower cap onto her head. She forced herself to forget about Hal. That, she reasoned, was long past—tonight there was a party. Taking a black cocktail dress from the closet, she moved to the floor-length mirror. She held the dress before her and studied the reflection. Pleased, she cocked her head to one side, feigning the icy pose of a fashion model. She placed the dress on the bed and stepped into the hallway with her towel.

Bronson was still stretched across the bed and, after finishing her bath, Claudia paused before his doorway. She watched his jaws, sunken and jaundiced, spread into a ludicrous grin and saw his bloodshot eyes widen in amazement as they focused on the top of her bathrobe, which she had purposefully left awry. He groped toward the foot of the bed, leaving a liquid trail after the bottle of cheap sherry that he still clutched. Claudia took a step closer and smiled. "Sweet thing," she whispered, then turned abruptly and, laughing aloud, returned to her room.

After dressing, she brushed her hair into a casual flip and returned to the mirror. She grinned—yes, as they had said, she was a fox. Again she'd be the center of attention. Her eyes moved up and down the mirror and, for a moment, the pallid grin faded and despite her looks she sensed that something had been lost. She poured another drink and, before leaving, finished it in a gulp. Outside, she ignored the murmured comments and whistles and, wavering slightly, made her way toward Lenox Avenue and a downtown cab.

A GATHERING OF ARTISTS
(FOR JOHN O. KILLENS
     GWENDOLYN BROOKS)

Seemingly,
(i) shall never
forget this night
    listening
    to you
    BEAUTIFUL CREATURES
    of pied-less beauty
    cursing and arguing
    at
       one
           an/other
                fool jumps-up and says,
                       shit hell goddamn universal
                       niggers humanity—shit
                       what about humanity.

ALICIA JOHNSON

175

and art
still remaining calm

        under this

                hyper-sensitive
                      tonic
                  individuals
              who are BLACK & BEAUTIFUL
                              love to love

(i) love to love freely
your smooth voice
with arrogant tones
            sweeping impatient
            rhythms into my
            naked-ear

and the smell
of scotch on
your breath
  is
A-R-T
  in
  its
natural form.

what makes
        (them   me)
(me   them)
us   we
  and
    i
use
these damn meaningless pronouns
at a time like this.

now sentences are born
a new man is discovered
a new art

      nurtured in us

cause (we) are
             beautiful people

with scotch &
water,
     pleasing each other
               we kiss &
               continue to curse
               on the rug of
                     no mannerism
tell me
what did you say
        a-b-o-u-t
            b-l-a-c-k
              w-o-M-A-N-h-o-o-d
and my senses
        become one with (yours)
           and
        here (i) go again
            getting
            into damn non sensual pronouns,

but baby
     ain't WE real tonite/
real again
real alive
us all and other pronouns
          we are
          crazy maniacs
          us all
          in the same
             damn boat/

but free
all up
        in HEAH,
at this
            BLACK GATHERING OF ARTISTS

James Brown, Hoodoo and Black Culture

CECIL BROWN

It is only recently that James Brown, the number-one soul-culture hero for millions of blacks, has attracted serious attention from black intellectuals and critics of black culture. Just a few years ago, when talking about black music, one spoke of the "serious" jazz musicians; now one can say that James Brown and Junior Walker are as complex as Ornette Coleman. A few years ago black "intellectuals" didn't dance to James Brown; but things have changed somewhat since then. Although one can still attend a number of parties given by blacks, say, in New York City and find people dancing to the Rolling Stones more often than JB, cutting into James Brown now seems to be the test of one's identity, of one's blackness. For a long time Brown's music, his style, his drama belonged to the masses of black people; now suddenly, almost unnoticeably, hip blacks from every social stratum are coming home to the "Popcorn" and "Ain't It Funky Now." What, really, is the cultural and artistic and political significance of this change?

During the urban riots, Brown went on the air with "cool it" messages, and for this he was criticized by blacks. But those were the times in which one had to be "politically relevant" in order to be black. If you weren't wearing a dashiki and telling black people what to do or telling black writers what to write; if you weren't cussing out the white liberal on television, you weren't black, you weren't politically relevant. With these definitions of blackness and politics, James Brown, basically a performer, was not popular with black intellectuals. The advent of Brown's acceptance by these people indicates a change in their political and cultural values.

What is becoming apparent is that Brown and artists like him are themselves examples of the positive aspects of black life. By being black in his art, Brown is saying that Doris Day and the Beatles and the Rolling Stones are simple-minded; when he does the funky-chicken, he is saying white people can't dance; when he confounds the music establishment with another new, totally different hit, he is saying the music resources of whites are limited and finite.

If black means anything nowadays, it means living honestly; and James Brown as an artist lives very clean. Selling wolf-tickets is not living clean—you got to put out. People are tired of hearing blacks talk about what they can do or are gonna do: people are tired of jiving—at least I am. Most people who are out there talking about what is or what is not black culture never produce one single poem, novel, painting or musical score. When they talk about black culture it is usually in the interest of politics and not art.

Brown then is a symbol of a new attitude toward black culture. Black thinkers are beginning to come around to the fact that, in the past, America has been interested only in the *conflict* between blacks, and have not wanted to hear about black people dealing beautifully with each other. Zora Neale Hurston was as fine a writer as Richard Wright, but because most of her writing was concerned with black folklore she never gained national attention. Like Hurston, Brown's reputation was made a long time before America (i.e., *Life*, *Look*, Ed Sullivan, etc.) got around to him. The conflict between blacks and whites may be termed protest art, but the relationship between blacks themselves, when expressed in art, is protest only indirectly. The first is ultimately an explanation, whereas the latter is the thing itself. James Brown is the real thing; soul is the real thing, which is why it is difficult to explain it. Blues is the real thing; Janis Joplin is an explanation. Nigger feeling is the real thing, the actual thing, the source; Negro leaders, black leaders are finally explanations, explainers, etc.

The spiritual source of Brown's music and style can be traced back, I think, to our hoodoo culture. (Hoodoo is the name given to voodoo by blacks in the South. By hoodoo culture I mean that black Southern culture in which people believed in "roots," "conjuring," "hoodoo doctors," etc.—i.e., "illiterate culture," the religion and art of the slave.) Historically, the elements of African religion, out of which hoodoo culture came, survived in the Negro church. The Negro church "was not at first by any means Christian," W. E. B. Du Bois tells us in *Souls of Black Folk*. "Rather it was an adaptation and mingling of heathen rites among the members of each plantation, and roughly designated as Voodooism."

Basic to African religion is the idea of multiple forces—not central force as in Christianity. The dead are forces, old people are forces and the living are forces. In primitive religion there is no such thing as good and evil in the moral sense—there are only forces with varying amounts of strength. This is still true to some extent in black American culture. The poem "Stagolee" is not considered vulgar by blacks; it is simply very powerful. Similarly, the sexuality of James Brown's music offends and repels only those blacks who have adopted class values that are moral in nature. Less "civilized" blacks find this quality of Brown's music "deep."

Linguistically, this aspect of African religion is more evident. For example, the force of black language, when used to describe the esthetic quality of a thing, usually moves downward (funky, heavy, it's a groove, deep, bad, down, in there, out there, out of sight, gone). This is essentially an Africanism; it has no moral bottom. It allows the black artist to stretch out, to *get down*.

Another element of African religion that survived in hoodoo is possession, the central element of Haitian voodoo. In voodoo and in hoodoo on a more symbolic level, a person can seduce a powerful force (gods, loas) into his body, and for a time he is that force. Note that in Christianity one *leaves* his body to go up to the force. In voodoo, one is with the force (god) *and* his body; whereas in Christianity one is without his body. Thus African spirituality sanctions body movement, body involvement, and this acceptance is basic to black culture and characteristic of James Brown's style. (My discussion of African religion is influenced by "The Mind of Africa," Janheinz Jahn (pp. 51–59), and "Munta," Janheinz Jahn.)

Hoodoo culture is not a visually oriented culture like Christianity. In the same manner black culture is opposed to a Christian, literate, visual definition; it is, like voodoo, pagan, oral, auditory. The disesteemed blacks that James Baldwin wrote about received their identity through the media, the printed word as image. On the other hand, in hoodoo culture, it is the image that surrounds you—*sound* —that defines. The way James Brown says "Good-God" is what defines the phrase, not its denotative meaning, but its tonetic quality. Specifically, what I am saying is that in hoodoo culture poems, novels and lyrics are not about things. They *are* things. A poem or play cannot be about the struggle—that's visual. The work has to *be* the struggle—that's hoodoo, magic. Content and style gotta be the same. Only then is it black art. Black is Being, black being (is).

When James Brown does his number about being black and proud, the thing that makes the song black art is not that it's about being black and proud, but that it *is* black and proud. The music-magic moves, transports you into a state of ecstatic joy and you feel the full life (magara) drilling your body and you think the words and the words alive—you be feeling good and then you *are* black and proud. When it goes away and you repeat the words to yourself, the words don't do it and you know you need JB and then you know you need the black artist who moves you and you wanna be moved and that's what it's all about.

In the way he uses lyrics Brown is very close to other black oral composers: the original blues people (the blues were never written when performed by blacks) or the creators and re-creators of old favorite ghetto epics like "The Titanic," "Signifying Monkey" and "Stagolee." What Brown's lyrics mean, as I have said, is determined not by the dictionary, but by how he makes it sound. Most of Brown's lyrics, for example, consist of guttural sounds that imitate physical lovemaking, and that's what those particular lyrics mean. Like the blues (didya ever listen to anybody try to "explain" the blues), the true Brown lyric doesn't have a "meaning" in the same way that a phrase such as "there was a man" has meaning. What, for instance, does "Mother Popcorn" mean? But what difference does it make when you are dancing to it, when you are feeling it, when you are it and it you (possession). It's nothing and everything at once; it is what black (hoodoo) people who never studied art in school mean by art.

> Bring it up, bring it up:
> Bring it up, bring it up.
> Can you do the jerk? Then watch me work.
> Can you do the slide? Then watch me glide.

Black (literary) poets can learn a lot from Brown, and I think that is becoming very apparent—despite the man's politics. Like oral blues singers before him, one thing he has brought into the media, the visual world, is the vernacular, which for so long the literary people were afraid to touch with a ten-foot pole. "Let a Man Come In and Do the Popcorn" is a beautiful stroke.

And in terms of politics, Brown has a kind of personal conviction that reminds one of Muhammad Ali: After denouncing Leslie Uggams and Robert Hooks on the Mike Douglas Show for being "Negroes," Brown was backed up by the FCC. Later Brown said, "They didn't have to back me up, I was right." About making a movie of his life, he goes on to say that "I'll play myself in my life story. All the real people will play themselves . . . I am an actor that is now."

An actor that is *now*. Elsewhere he said: "Everyday is history for me." There is no memory because nothing is forgotten; there is no distinction between past and future, it is all now. It envelops you and touches you and you can touch it and feel it and you don't need an explanation to enjoy it. It's art, honest black art that *is* the new political awareness. In the future all the real people will play themselves.

Like the man said, there's more to being black than meets the *eye*.

Notes About the Authors

BARRY BECKHAM has had articles published in *Esquire, New York* magazine, and *The New York Times*. His novel, *My Main Mother,* was published in 1969. He is currently a visiting lecturer at Brown University, his alma mater.

ED BULLINS, a playwright, co-founded Black Arts/West in San Francisco's Fillmore District and is a member of the Black Arts Alliance. He is resident playwright of the New Lafayette Theatre in Harlem and the editor of *Black Theatre.* A collection of his plays has been published as well as a four-act play, *The Duplex.*

CECIL BROWN is the author of the novel *The Life and Loves of Mr. Jiveass Nigger.* He is currently working on the screenplay for *Jiveass Nigger* and has completed an original play entitled *Our Sisters Are Pregnant.*

DAVID SCOTT BROWN is a graduate of Pratt Institute and is employed on the art staff of *The New York Times.* He has had several one-man shows.

CAROLE CLEMMONS is a native of Youngstown, Ohio. Her poetry has appeared in the anthology *Nine Black Poets.* She is now living and working in New York City.

GEORGE DAVIS, a former United States Air Force pilot, has worked as a reporter for the *Washington Post* and as an editor for *The New York Times* Drama Section. His fiction has appeared in *Negro Digest* (*Black World*) and *Amistad 1*. His first novel, focused on the Vietnam war, will be published later this year.

NIKKI GIOVANNI is a graduate of Fisk University and has published two volumes of poetry, *Black Feeling, Black Talk* and *Black Judgement*. She is now living in New York City and teaching at Rutgers University, Livingston College.

DAVID HENDERSON, one of the founders of *Umbra,* a black literary magazine, has been poet in residence at the College of the City of New York and the University of California at Berkeley. He has published two collections of poetry: *Felix and the Silent Forest* and *De Mayor of Harlem*.

FRANKLIN JACKSON is a native of Memphis, Tennessee, now living in New York City. "Claudia" is excerpted from a novel in progress.

ALICIA JOHNSON is a Chicago-based poet whose works have appeared in *Nommo, Negro Digest* (*Black World*), and the anthology *Nine Black Poets*.

GEORGE KENT, a professor of English at the University of Chicago, holds an M.A. and Ph.D. degree from Boston University and has been a college dean as well as an editorial associate on a poetry journal.

JULIUS LESTER's most recent books are *Black Folktales* and *Search for the New Land*. His biography and anthology of the writings of W.E.B. DuBois, *Seventh Son,* will soon be published. Lester's articles and reviews have appeared regularly in *Evergreen Review* and *The New York Times Book Review*. He is the moderator of WBAI-FM talk show.

REGINALD MAJOR is the director of San Francisco State College's Educational Opportunity Program. "Who Shall Rule the Jungle" is taken from his book, *A Panther Is a Black Cat*.

SHANE STEVENS' first novel, *Go Down Dead,* was published in 1967; his second novel, *Way Uptown in Another World,* will appear this year. His articles have appeared in numerous publications and he has taught at Bread Loaf.

MEL WATKINS is a graduate of Colgate University. His articles and reviews have appeared in *New Leader, Essence, Amistad 2,* and *Nickel Review.* He is co-editor of *To Be a Black Woman: Portraits in Fact and Fiction.*

EDGAR WHITE, a native of the West Indies, was raised in Harlem. His plays have been performed at The New York Shakespeare Festival Public Theater and at the Eugene O'Neill Foundation. Both his fiction and drama have appeared in *Liberator* magazine and he has recently published a collection of plays entitled *Underground.*

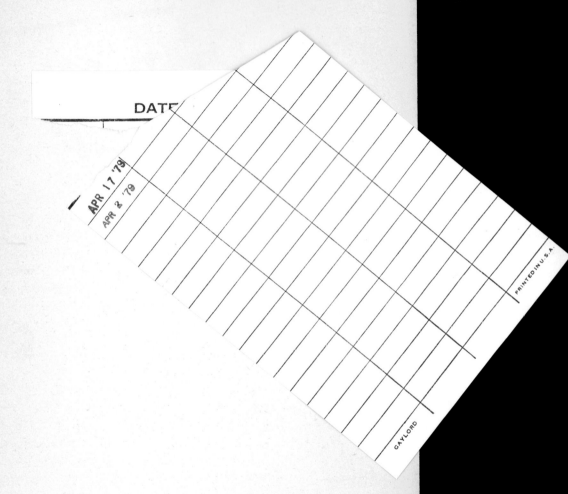